TAROT READING FOR BEGINNERS

The #1 Guide to Psychic Tarot Reading, Real Tarot Card Meanings & Tarot Divination Spreads—Master the Art of Reading the Cards and Discover their True Meaning

By Shelly O'Bryan

© Copyright 2019 by Shelly O'Bryan - All rights reserved.

This content is provided with the sole purpose of providing relevant information on a specific topic for which every reasonable effort has been made to ensure that it is both accurate and reasonable. Nevertheless, by purchasing this content you consent to the fact that the author, as well as the publisher, are in no way experts on the topics contained herein, regardless of any claims as such that may be made within. As such, any suggestions or recommendations that are made within are done so purely for entertainment value. It is recommended that you always consult a professional prior to undertaking any of the advice or techniques discussed within.

This is a legally binding declaration that is considered both valid and fair by both the Committee of Publishers Association and the American Bar Association and should be considered as legally binding within the United States.

The reproduction, transmission, and duplication of any of the content found herein, including any specific or extended information will be done as an illegal act regardless of the end form the information ultimately takes. This includes copied versions of the work both physical, digital and audio unless express consent of the Publisher is provided beforehand. Any additional rights reserved.

Furthermore, the information that can be found within the pages described forthwith shall be considered both accurate and truthful when it comes to the recounting of facts. As such, any use, correct or incorrect, of the provided information will render the Publisher free of responsibility as to the actions taken outside of their direct purview. Regardless, there are zero scenarios where the original author or the Publisher can be deemed liable in any fashion for any damages or hardships that may result from any of the information discussed herein.

Additionally, the information in the following pages is intended only for informational purposes and should thus be thought of as universal. As befitting its nature, it is presented without assurance regarding its prolonged validity or interim quality. Trademarks that are mentioned are done without written consent and can in no way be considered an endorsement from the trademark holder.

TABLE OF CONTENTS

Introduction 1
Chapter 1 *The History Of Tarot*.. 3
Chapter 2 *On Decks*.. 9
Chapter 3 *Major Arcana, The Fool – The Wheel Of Fortune* 13
Chapter 4 *Major Arcana, Justice – The World* 31
Chapter 5 *Minor Arcana, The Pips* 47
Chapter 6 *Minor Arcana, The Court Cards* 61
Chapter 7 *Spreads* 69
Chapter 8 *Reading With Context* 81
Chapter 9 *The Role Of Intuition* 88
Chapter 10 *Exercises & Practice* 93
Conclusion 99
Description for Book 101
Description for Audio Book 102

INTRODUCTION

Most people know the word tarot, or at least have heard it before. They know it's a deck of cards of some kind, and that psychics on TV will lay them out on a table with their crystal ball and incense and clutch their chest at what they see. It seems very mysterious when viewed through that lens. However, tarot is rarely so dramatic.

The first thing that needs to be said: you do not have to psychic to read the tarot. It takes intuition to read it to its fullest potential, but intuition is an ability everyone has, whether they know it or not. Being psychic is a culmination of intuitive gifts, and if you are, it will certainly help. But any average person on the street could learn to read tarot if they wanted to. It's a splendidly therapeutic way to work through your problems. When we ask a question of the cards and lay them out for a reading, we're accessing a part of us that doesn't speak in words but in feelings and subconscious nudges, we sense all the time but usually ignore. Tarot puts images to those nudges and gives words to the messages we need to hear. It brings our intuition front and center so we can confront our issues head-on. It is this intuition that allows us to read for others as well. As your abilities develop with practice, you'll find your readings becoming clearer and clearer, no psychic abilities needed.

In this book, we'll introduce you, the reader, to this system of intuitive divination that is tarot. While not like TV, it is very enlightening and can aid you in furthering yourself on your personal journey.

In the first chapter, we will go over the history of the tarot and reveal the source of its more esoteric symbolism.

Secondly, we will go over how to choose a deck for yourself.

From there, in the third and fourth chapter, we'll go over the meanings of each individual card in the Major Arcana. This has been split into two chapters so you can navigate through them quicker when you need to go back and look up meanings for a reading.

The fifth and sixth chapters are about the Minor Arcana. First, we'll go over numerical cards, also known as pips. Next, we'll go over the Court cards, the Kings, Queens, Knights, and the Pages of the deck.

The seventh chapter is all about spreads. Several are offered in this book as a launching point for you to explore different ways to read the cards.

We go over how to read the cards within the context of the question in the eighth chapter. This is one of the most important elements of sound card reading.

The ninth discusses the other most important element, the role of intuition. Here, we talk about why it's so important for tarot reading and methods of improving your intuition.

Finally, in the tenth chapter, we'll provide exercises you can do on your own in lieu of a querent to read for in order to practice reading. This chapter will also provide some ideas for online sources to explore to further your studies.

With this book, we hope to help ease you into reading the cards in an easy, respectful manner, where you can develop at your own pace. This book aims to be your guide as you learn everything and to be a resource to refer back to once you're reading regularly and need supplemental advice. It takes a while to memorize all the cards, so don't be surprised if you find yourself referring back for clarification even after a few years of experience under your belt.

It can be overwhelming at first to approach everything there is to learn from the tarot. It's not surprising that it's confused more than a few initiates at first. If it seems daunting, don't give up. Put your deck away for a day or two, clear your head, and come back to it when you've processed what you've learned until you're ready to continue. Once learned, the tarot will be a lifetime aid for your journey through this life, so there's no rush.

CHAPTER 1
The History Of Tarot

Where the tarot came from is a topic as full of mysticism as the cards themselves. On one hand, its existence is tied up with the average deck of playing cards, and on the other, with deep hermetic philosophy regarding alchemy, astrology, and the Kabbalah. But how far back the tarot actually goes is a question of mystery.

What historians know for certain is the earliest deck of cards that we know of resembling the tarot hails from the mid-15th century, and as far as we know, was used purely as a system of trick-taking games. These games, known by the name *tarot* in France, *tarocchi* in Italy, and *tarock* in Germany, are still played to this day in non-English speaking countries around Europe. These decks had four suits with numbers cards known as pips and a series of trump cards which varied depending on the region. Because printing wasn't in existence yet, each of these original decks were hand-painted and often commissioned by wealthy families, with the trump cards featuring members of that family.

Over time, and especially when the printing press became widespread, these decks were modified to fit the most popular games played in each region of Europe. Most slimmed down a lot and became what we recognize as the standard 52-card deck we play with today, with only the Fool remaining as the Joker card, and the Wands, Cups, Swords, and Pentacles suits morphing into clubs, hearts, spades, and diamonds. It is primarily the French *tarot* that kept all original twenty-two trumps and the original suits, and that is what came over into the English-speaking world under that name.

It was in 1781 when a pastor by the name of Antoine Court de Gébelin wrote a compilation of essays called *The Primeval World, Analyzed and Compared to the Modern World*. Within this massive text, a chapter deals with tarot interpretations, and it is here that the notion of the tarot being associated with hermetic ideology was first published.

Court de Gébelin claimed that the tarot was a distillation of the ancient Egyptian Book of Thoth, a legendary compendium of wisdom supposedly written by the gods. According to Court to Gébelin, all the knowledge and secrets of these hermetic texts were translated into the specific images of the trump cards in the tarot as a shorthand for spiritual insight. The figures represented different aspects of alchemy, astrology, and Kabbalah mysticism. He also claimed that the Catholic Church was well aware of the tarot's magical properties and worked to deliberately keep the knowledge locked away.

There is some truth to this in the fact that playing cards did originate from Egypt and were brought over to Europe in the 1500s, which is when the *tarot, tarocchi,* and *tarock* decks appeared. However, Court de Gébelin never produced any real historical evidence that the playing cards the *tarot* were based on were anything more than games to the Egyptians, either.

Despite the lack of evidence, his work stirred a lot of interest, and after his writings circulated around a bit, an occultist named Etteilla stepped forward with more to say on the subject. Etteilla had already published a book in 1770. *Etteilla or A Way to Entertain Yourself with a Deck of Cards* outlined a method of cartomancy using playing cards. In 1785, he wrote another book, *How to Entertain Yourself with the Deck of Cards called Tarot*, as a direct response to Court de Gébelin's 1781 work. In it, he claimed he had learned his methods of cartomancy from an Italian fortune-teller as far back as 1751, lending credence the motion that the tarot cards held more meaning than just as games for a long time. He then offered methods of tarot divination to support this idea. By 1790, Etteilla had reworked the tarot to incorporate the hermetic principles more clearly and created the first deck of tarot cards made specifically for divination purposes.

It was this tarot and not the trick-taking game *tarot* that made its way to Victorian England. Interest in the occult and spiritual practices were becoming more popular there during that time, so many people took the ideas started by Court de Gébelin and Etteilla and developed them further. By the end of the 19th century, mysticism and tarot had irrevocably merged. Occult groups formed around these studies, mostly secret societies who wished to keep this knowledge secret from any except for initiates who proved they could fully comprehend them.

The most famous of these was the Hermetic Order of the Golden Dawn. This was a spiritualist society of the rich and famous based out of Great Britain. Of its many noteworthy members, the two that are most famous for their contribution to the tarot is Arther Edward Waite and Aleister Crowley. Both created decks that heavily influenced the modern tarot, which we will go over in Chapter 2. It was their contributions that fully cemented the ancient Egyptian connections of Thoth and spiritualism to the tarot, and gave us the tarot as we know it today.

The tarot's popularity died down for a while through the 20th century and was seen mostly as an esoteric interest. It was difficult to find decks or books on the subject. But in recent years, the tarot has seen a resurgence of popularity, mostly due to its accessibility on the internet. Now, any deck can be found from anywhere in the world, and dozens upon dozens of resources are available to learn more about it at the click of a mouse. Once an object of superstition meant for fortune tellers and occult practitioners, it has seen an immense amount of interest out of its capacity to be used for self-discovery. As we will see in later chapters, the meanings of the cards can be applied to a wide variety of problems and emotional traumas and can be used not just for games, not just for divination, but as a means for the growth of the Self.

Whether or not tarot truly did come from ancient Egypt disguised as playing cards as Etteilla and Court de Gébelin claimed, the idea has become so infused in the design of the tarot and how people think about it that it might as well be taken into full account. We've already mentioned a couple of times the term 'hermetic.' The subject of hermeticism is too dense to tackle in this book to its conclusion. However, as it relates to the tarot, it is an important subject to at least introduce.

The word 'hermetic' comes from writings attributed to one called Hermes Trismegistus. This supposed author was long thought to be a contemporary of Moses, though, with modern understanding, it is improbable this person ever existed as flesh and blood. It's more likely the writings were a compilation of different authors over a period of time. These texts, known collectively as the *Hermetica*, focus on Oneness with the Divine. It touches on a range of subjects such as astrology, alchemy, and occult magic. This philosophy had a huge impact on the development of what we call the West today and the Arabic world and inspired many from theologians to scientists with its approach to skepticism of the physical and development of the spiritual.

The *Hermetica* is dated back to the 1st century AD. However, many argue that their origins actually come from far further in the past, stating this knowledge was passed down through oral tradition and lost texts for centuries before being written in the form we know it today. Some say they came from ancient Greece, while others go even further and claim it was the ancient Egyptians who penned these revelations down. This gets even muddier since the Greek god Hermes was often compared with the Egyptian god Thoth during the Hellenistic period, as they were both mythical representatives of writing and knowledge, and so some use that to support the idea that Hermes Trimegistus was both gods combined into a figure of wisdom during a much older era.

Since Court de Gébelin tied the tarot to ancient Egypt, he imbued it with the hermetic philosophy associated with it, though due to the time in which he was writing, most of the Greek and Egyptian elements were Christianized. It was through this lens that he gave the tarot its heavier weight as a spiritual tool for Europeans and not just pretty cards to bet with.

He also tied it closely with the Kabbalah. This is another extremely esoteric school of thought, this time coming from ancient Judaism. Like hermeticism, Kabbalah is cosmically dense and spans far too much history and theology to adequately describe here. The main thing about the Kabbalah as it relates to the tarot is the symbol of the Tree of Life. This is a diagram consisting of ten nodes, known as sephiroth, that are connected by a system of paths. It describes the realization of the Divine to the Mundane—or, in other words, pure consciousness manifesting into the earthly realm through a series of balanced but opposite transformations. It is considered to be a map of creation.

The sephiroth represent a wide variety of things in the Kabbalah tradition, ranging from angelic beings to colors to numbers, and have Hebrew names that represent their function. In the tarot, the pip cards in the Minor Arcana embody the energy of each sephirah. For example, the Aces (talked about in Chapter 5) are associated with Kether, the first sephiroth in the Tree of Life. Kether is the abstract, intangible potential for being, the Crown of the Tree of Life, and the Aces embody that as they are the potential of their respective suits.

The Major Arcana represent the pathways between the sephiroth. These paths show the relationship between the sephiroth and how the Divine must move from one to the other and are symbolized by Hebrew letters. By placing the tarot as symbols for these paths and giving them the Hebrew association, Court de Gébelin and the occultists who followed after him sought to put a face to these paths so we may know what actions to take in our spiritual quests as we move from one phase to another.

This is pretty complicated, so don't worry if it seems a little out there. For a beginner, all this hermetic and Kabbalah symbolism has little effect on your ability to read the cards. You're encouraged to go study more into these subjects if you're interested. Copies of the *Hermetica* are available on Amazon for free or next to nothing. *The Kybalion* is also a hermetic text that may be of interest to you. If you want to read more about Kabbalah, the most essential text is the *Zohar*, a mystical commentary on the Kabbalah tradition written in medieval times. It is considered crucial for understanding the fundamentals of Kabbalah, outside of reading the ancient Hebrew Torah.

We only touch on all this because, due to the influence of the Order of the Golden Dawn, the tarot has taken on this groundwork for its symbolism and become a vessel for meaning. A lot of the symbols in older tarot decks, like the Rider Waite-Smith or the Thoth, use alchemical and astrological symbolism in their cards to get across these hermetic meanings.

It's important for anyone who gets into tarot to know there is so much more below the surface. Here, we merely aim to lay the groundwork if you decide to explore this history further. Whether or not the tarot originally came from ancient Egypt, those ancient philosophies are now a part of its history. The meanings these hermetic traditions gave the cards still influence artists who create decks, and the readers who glean meaning from them.

CHAPTER 2
On Decks

Let's move on and discuss the most important piece of this whole process: the deck itself. As with any skill, acquiring the right tools is key to development. Choosing your tarot deck is as important a step of learning the meanings of the cards. What many don't realize at first is just how many decks exist. Dozens of different varieties are in circulation and it can get overwhelming when you're a beginner.

Firstly, where does one acquire a deck? The first place to look is at a metaphysical store, sometimes called crystal shops. These stores sell products geared towards Wicca practitioners and modern witches and offer crystals, stones, incense, candles, besoms, angel medallions, and of course, divination decks.

Tarot is widely commercially available, though, if a metaphysical store is not nearby. Big box stores like Barnes & Noble have a whole spiritual section that sells decks alongside books on the subject. They don't have as many as some metaphysical stores do, but it's a good place to start if there are no crystal shops in your area.

Of course, there is always the internet. Amazon has a wide variety in their catalog, and there are online stores specializing in divination decks that can be found with a quick search. It's also possible to get them straight from the publishers. U.S. Games and Llewellyn Worldwide are the two main companies who publish decks in the U.S. and they have all their decks available for order right on their site.

The great thing about the internet, though, is stumbling upon something that isn't widely available, and tarot decks have seen such a resurgence in popularity that many artists have self-published their own decks. It takes some digging to find these indie decks, but the variety of styles and the beauty of some of them makes it worthwhile. Joining a tarot forum can point you in the right direction as there are many avid deck collectors who spend a lot of time searching for just these types of tarot art.

The general rule of buying a tarot deck is to go with the one you feel drawn to. Much of reading depends on interpreting the images on the cards, so if you hate the art, it's likely you're going to hate reading the deck. There's also the more mystical element of feeling the energy of the deck. It's a common phenomenon for readers to describe their decks as if they have distinct personalities. Some work with you and some don't, much like people, and there's nothing more frustrating than buying a deck only to realize it's difficult to work with. When picking a deck to learn the tarot, it's important to get the one that feels right for you. Don't over-analyze, just go with your intuition.

That said, it is recommended that you consider the Rider Waite-Smith Tarot as your first deck. The Rider Waite-Smith, designed by A.E. Waite and illustrated by Pamela Coleman Smith, serves as the basis for the design of most decks available now. It's difficult to understate just how influential this deck is. It turned the pip cards into clean, clear illustrated designs that reflect the cartomancy meaning for ease of reading, and it was instrumental in making the tarot approachable, bringing it out of the hands of esoteric mystics and into the public sphere. It is the most widely available deck in the world. Any store that sells tarot will have this deck, guaranteed. If you can read the Rider Waite-Smith, you'll have an easier time learning to read the dozens of other decks that follow its example. So if you're having trouble deciding on a deck, it's a good bet to go with this one.

Another important deck to note is from A.E. Waite's fellow occultist, Aleister Crowley. He is the creator of the Thoth Tarot along with artist Lady Frieda Harris. This is a much more ambitious deck, steeped in the deeply esoteric mythology and astrology of the Order of the Golden Dawn. Generally, it's only recommended you get this deck if you're an advanced reader interested in exploring the deeper mysticism of the tarot, as it is notoriously difficult to read for divination. It's only brought up here because some modern decks are influenced by its focus on Kabbalah hermeticism and anyone getting into tarot should be aware of it. Again, go with your gut, but generally speaking, any deck designed after the Rider Waite-Smith will be a more approachable than one following in the footsteps of the Thoth deck.

Whatever the deck, every tarot pack has seventy-eight cards, with twenty-two Major Arcana and fifty-six Minor Arcana. Every Major Arcana has the same archetypes, starting with the Fool and ending with the World, and every Minor Arcana is split into four suits with fourteen cards each. Tarot is a very rigid system with this very specific structure to the deck design. It can get confusing when looking at decks for the first time, but keep in mind that any deck that does not have this structure is not tarot. There are other divination card systems, but they all have their own separate symbolism and are read very differently. Lenormand is not tarot. Kipper is not tarot. Oracle cards are not tarot. They are very interesting systems and you are encouraged to explore them as well, but this book will not help you to understand them.

Then what's the difference between all the tarot decks available? Simply put, it's in the way the artist decided to interpret the meanings of each card.

Often the way these decks will set themselves apart from each other is through a theme. For example, a very popular deck is the Wildwood Tarot, which uses Celtic influence and nature as its imagery. Even though it is based on the Rider Waite-Smith tarot, the image on the card in this deck is usually not the same as the corresponding card in the Rider Waite-Smith deck. Sometimes, the cards are even renamed to suit the theme. In the Wildwood Tarot, the High Priestess from the Rider-Waite is renamed the Seer, and the Hierophant is called the Ancestor.

Even more, changes can be seen from deck to deck. Sometimes the Wands suit is called Rods, or the Pentacles are Disks or Coins. A Page in one deck is called Princess in another, or Daughter in yet another. Some decks remove the imagery completely from European tradition and places it instead in the context of another culture with all the mythical correlations included. However, even with these changes, the meaning of the cards remains the same, and the underlying structure of the tarot stays intact—still seventy-eight cards, still a Major and Minor Arcana, still four suits. What's different is how the message through the cards comes across.

Usually, though, tarot decks stick to tradition and keep the old names, instead of using imagery alone to provide new perspectives.

That is why it is so important to choose a deck you connect with as far as the artwork is concerned. The art helps you unlock the meanings of each card and how they connect together to give you a picture of what's going on in your reading. We'll go more into why this is when we discuss reading the cards with intuition in Chapter 9.

There is also the option of making your own deck. There are blank sets you can buy that are ready to be drawn on and used right away. If you're really crafty, though, all you need is card stock, a paper slicer, and a corner cutter. Then you can create them to be any size you want. If you draw your own interpretations of the cards, it will resonate that much more since you'll know exactly what the imagery means and why you picked it. It's a very magical process worth exploring for anyone with a knack for artistic expression. It helps to be familiar with the cards first, to know their meanings and how they work together, but tarot doesn't need to be elaborate, detailed art.

Whatever deck you decide on, take it out while we go through the fundamentals of the card's meanings. Let the cards speak to you while you learn.

CHAPTER 3
Major Arcana, The Fool – The Wheel Of Fortune

The word 'arcana' is the plural of 'arcanum,' and means mysterious, specialized knowledge. It is frequently associated with alchemy, which sought to transmute the disparate elements of nature into something purified and immortal, most famously gold. Within the tarot, then, we get two sets of secret knowledge, the Major Arcana and the Minor Arcana. Through them, as alchemists of the soul, we can synthesize the pieces of ourselves into spiritual gold, an elixir of life that is not a literal drink but the Fountain of Life that comes from within.

The Major Arcana deals with grand, overarching concepts. Each card represents an archetype of the universe or the human condition. They signify deep occultist symbolism, and on their own can be intimately studied for their mystical weight. For the purposes of divination, though, their main significance is emphasizing a point in a reading. If a Major Arcana card shows up, it's usually telling the reader, "This is important. Pay attention."

We will discuss the meanings of the Major Arcana using the Fool's Journey. This is a model of exploring the cards by visualizing the sequence of the cards as a story, one in which we all start as inexperienced fools but, by taking this Journey, we become one with the world. It is the tale of the soul becoming whole.

Each card will be described first by it's heavier, more spiritual implications, followed by the divinatory meanings for quick reference in your readings. The corresponding astrological associations and Kabbalic attributes will also be listed with each card. This is so if you decide to fall down the tarot rabbit-hole of hermetic philosophy, you'll already have an idea of each card's connotation in your studies.

Each card of the Major Arcana has a positive and negative context. In this book, we will call the negative the card's shadow aspect. Some call this ill-dignified, or how some readers read reversals. We will discuss reversals and dignities in Chapter 8, but for now, read the shadow aspect as part of the card's overall messages and meanings.

A note on the numbers of the Major Arcana: as discussed in the previous chapter, all tarot decks have the same number of cards and use the same meanings for each card. However, some decks have the card Strength as VIII and Justice as XI, while others switched them around. This has to do with the Rider Waite-Smith. Traditionally, because tarot had so much connection to the Kabbalic mysteries, the cards were numbered based on where they lay on the Tree of Life. This places Justice as VIII and Strength as XI. However, A.E. Waite decided to switch them for his deck to align more with their astrological significance. For the general reader, this has little consequence. It is only mentioned here because this book follows the Rider Waite-Smith model of Strength as VIII and Justice as XI since that deck is standard for most. If your deck has them the other way, it is not a misprint, it was a choice of the deck designer.

In this chapter, we will go through the first half of the Major Arcana. This is the Fool's Journey through the Mundane Realm. All the figures we will meet here are the archetypes of humanity. Here exist the aspects of the Divine Feminine and the Divine Masculine. Here, our relationships to the external world around us are challenged and explored, and the way these influences reflect how we relate to ourselves. By exploring the Mundane Realm, we develop the spiritual fortitude and knowledge we need to turn within. We must come to understand the elements of our nature if we are to transmute them into something greater.

0 - The Fool
Alchemical Association: Elemental Air
Kabbalah Path: Aleph, the Ox

This is the beginning of the Journey, and paradoxically, its end as well. As the number zero suggests, it is unlimited potential, the vacuum which all things come and all things seek to balance back to.

Often, the imagery in this card depicts a youth about to step off a cliff with his gaze up to the sky, heedless or willfully ignorant of the chasm before him. Like Joseph Campbell's hero, the Fool represents us as we are, ignorant of the greater forces at work and yet moving forward to find our place in the universe anyway. It brings to light the foolhardy bliss in walking along our paths. Despite all planning and foresight, life will take us where it takes us, and often, there is nothing we can do but embrace the mystery and follow it, knowing we may never understand its true nature.

But this card is not one of despair at the hands of fate. It is a celebration in taking the first steps to self-discovery regardless of failures or successes, doubts or joys. The ending is not what matters, for you cannot know it anyway. Beginning the Journey at all—that is what holds consequence.

Meanings: This is a positive card of affirmation. It is often a sign that something is coming in and that it is time to enter a new cycle in your life. This is the radical opportunity that comes along that makes you wonder if you're crazy for even thinking about it. Even more than the Aces (discussed in Chapter 6), the Fool says go for it, no matter what anyone else says or what doubts you may have over you. Take the chance and throw yourself off the cliff. You never know where you may end up, or more importantly, how you will change because of it.

Shadow Aspect: Sometimes, this card indicates genuine foolhardiness. Taking action is important, but if abused, it can lead to a brash attitude that will throw you around without any more enlightenment than you had before. It all comes down to timing. If this card comes up in shadow aspect, take a step back, evaluate your actions, and be patient. A true opportunity will come when it's ready.

I - The Magician
Astrological Association: Mercury
Kabbalah Path: Beth, the House

As above, so below; as below, so above. This phrase, divined centuries ago by the hermetic thinkers of the ancient past, encapsulates the power of the Magician. It expresses the hermetic principle of correspondence, which states that one reality is a reflection of all realities, and any action taken in one is also expressed through the others. The macrocosm of the universe is reflected in the microcosm of the Self, and vice versa. Thus, if you can understand one, you can understand the other.

The first aspect of the Divine Masculine, this card shows the will of the Self over the external. He is creative action, one who exerts influence not by bending the world to his will but by reflecting the world. He manifests that which is within himself into the reality around him, and in return, the world manifests something greater than himself within him.

The Magician invites you to align yourself with the universe and to find liberation in that unity. It is a jolt of energy that will set the Journey rolling forward through whatever may come.

Meanings: Whatever big ideas or plans you may have conceived before, the universe has aligned to help you bring them to fruition. All the little steps and setbacks that may arise are inconsequential in the face of your will to manifest your dreams into reality. Take action. Now is the time.

Shadow Aspect: The kind of unconscious creation exemplified by the Magician does not come with an innate conscience. Manifesting the life you want can lead to the unexpected, and sometimes that comes with folly or outright immorality. Many tarot readers have nicknamed this card 'The Trickster' due to its associations with questionable deeds. While upending the status quo once in a while can bring in a breath of fresh air, wrecking everything around you to force change will only lead to self-defeat. Make sure your intentions come from the aligned Self and not from personal gain before you take further action.

II – The High Priestess
Astrological Association: The Moon
Kabbalah Path: Gimel, the Camel

One of the most mysterious cards of the Major Arcana, the High Priestess carries a subtlety that only exemplifies her deeper meaning. A. E. Waite described her as, in some respects, "the highest and holiest of the Great Arcana."

The first aspect of the Divine Feminine, she is in many ways the personification of mystery. She sits in balance between the conscious and the subconscious, the tangible and the supernal, and acts as a conduit between them. She is often depicted in front of a veil, but her meanings actually place her *as* the veil between us and the enigma behind it. She holds the truth, but she is the truth as well. She reflects the light and so she is the light. What is hidden can be revealed, and what is revealed can be hidden, much like the phases of the moon with which she is so closely associated.

Because her riddles can't be gleaned through rational thought, the High Priestess requires your intuition for true understanding. Through silence, she tells you to tap into the knowledge you have without knowing how you have it and urges you to listen closely. Half of the Journey takes place within.

Meanings: When the High Priestess shows in a reading, there is an indication that not all aspects can be spelled out for you. Intuition and wisdom are the key to unlocking further knowledge. Rather than searching through outside sources, retreat within. Feel out the situation intuitively and let your gut guide you. Sometimes you already have the answers you need. Have faith in that.

Shadow Aspect: At times, this card reveals the presence of secrets or hidden agendas. In this case, there's a need for open and honest communication to reveal what is being kept from you, or what you may be keeping from others. As always, though, when it comes to the High Priestess, do so with empathy and guided intuition. It is through quiet contemplation that we can hear the smallest whispers.

III – The Empress
Astrological Association: Venus
Kabbalah Path: Daleth, the Door

The second aspect of the Divine Feminine, the Empress embodies abundance. She is the representation of Mother Earth, this Garden of Paradise we have been given. She is life itself flowing in sheer abandon.

Bounty and pleasure is a significant interpretation of this card. She is the creative energy of the higher love in all things expressed through the material plane. When the world is experienced through full awareness of the present moment, that is the Empress manifesting. The physical world is not separate from the higher realm but an expression of it, one that needs to be understood as a part of spiritual development. It is through our physical senses, through understanding our bodies and our world, that we can achieve greater knowledge beyond what we can see. It is the platform from which we can spring off into higher consciousness, and our safeguard when we swim out too deep and need rest. It is important to take care of our physical selves.

As your Journey takes you through the plentiful garden that is Earth, the Empress will be there to hold your hand when things seem overwhelming, and to remind you to stop, take a break if you need to, and stop to smell the flowers.

Meanings: The Empress comes when nurturing is needed. Look around. Take a walk and enjoy nature. Express yourself creatively. Make something beautiful. She is love personified, so let it flow from you and into you through self-care and supporting others. Through her, there is more than enough to go around. The Empress can also represent motherhood itself, or someone who exemplifies these qualities.

Shadow Aspect: Sometimes overindulgence can do more harm than good. Taking time to appreciate the pleasures in life is critical, but without discipline, it's easy to slip into laziness and inertia. In a negative context, this card may be showing that's exactly what's going on, whether it be you or someone in your life who is taking advantage of your love. Focus your creative power. It may be time to leave the garden and take on a challenge.

IV – The Emperor
Astrological Association: Aries
Kabbalah Path: Heh, the Window

If the Empress was the Holy Mother, here we have her counterpart, the Holy Father, the second aspect of the Divine Masculine. He is the hand that pushes us out of the nest.

Discipline makes up the center feature of this card's message. Unlike the Magician, who creates through reflecting a higher purpose, or the creative power inherent in the Empress, the Emperor is creation through the force of will. He provides rules to live by and then enforces them for our own good. In many ways, he is a representation of government and personifies how it creates a structure so we may live our lives in a productive manner rather than running through rampant chaos. He protects by providing a means to succeed. At times, it may seem harsh, but this strict approach enables us to learn how to stand on our own two feet.

In your Journey, he's there to encourage you to get out there and make something of yourself. It is a form of love that does not coddle because he knows you are capable of more. He will hold you to a higher standard and push you along when you get too comfortable. Through his leadership, you can be assured that you will complete your Journey.

Meanings: First and foremost, this card brings indications of authority. Structure, order, and recognition are brought to light with the Emperor. His message is fairness through a firm hand, and the respect that kind of power can bring if used wisely. It can also represent more literally a strong leader or father figure.

Shadow Aspect: This card also presents the danger of burning out. It takes a lot of energy to wield this much power—if not controlled or allowed to rest, it can very easily turn violent and destroy what was created. This is the leader who no longer knows how to lead. Perhaps all the focus and intent you're putting into a project is doing more harm than good. Ease up. Let go of control and accept that while your energy was needed to create, it does not require your strict attention anymore to sustain.

V – The Hierophant
Astrological Association: Taurus
Kabbalah Path: Vav, the Nail

Unlike the Emperor, who extols the virtues of strict discipline, or the High Priestess, who speaks of the hidden spirit within each of us, the Hierophant preaches salvation through dogma. He is not governing or guiding intuition. He is the exoteric promise of theology and the whisper of culture in our ear.

The Hierophant enforces the orthodox traditions of society. He is the keeper of where we have come from, and through the accumulated wisdom of the ages, he provides valuable insight. He is the teacher who guards the sacred. In return, those who seek to learn must follow the doctrine of the sacred and be willing to admit ignorance seeking knowledge.

The Hierophant provides the fundamental principles that will guide you further on your Journey than you thought possible. He can point out the pitfalls in your path and show you shortcuts you never would have noticed. Through his teachings and your humility, there is an opportunity to learn greater spiritual knowledge than you could ever learn on your own. You only need to be willing to follow his word.

Meanings: This card's most immediate symbolism brings to mind religion and spiritual beliefs. It can also mean other institutions who require obedience to tradition, such as school or a court. The Hierophant is what's tried-and-true, not innovation. Find a mentor or an establishment that can help you delve into study. Take the opportunity to grow under guidance. Once you lay down the groundwork what has already been discovered, then further learning can be reached.

Shadow Attributes: The hierarchical leadership portrayed in the Hierophant can take on a sadistic aspect if abused. A good teacher should aid their students in going further than they themselves have reached. Traditions are the ground upon which we can build progress, not the end-all-be-all. Holding knowledge back only impedes that process and can damage the student. Don't follow blindly—if your teacher cannot teach you, regain personal freedom and seek your own path.

VI – The Lovers
Astrological Association: Gemini
Kabbalah Path: Zain, the Sword

As the name suggests, the Lovers portray simple human love. Romantic love is the first thing that comes to mind, but it also represents the deep love we can feel in all relationships. It is our human connection with each other. It is the card of wholeness.

Lovers is one of the most difficult cards to interpret. It's immediate meaning is obvious, but there are many layers to this card that require deeper scrutiny. While the imagery of the Lovers depicts the joy in coming together, it's inherent implication is that there was a separation in the first place. By being two instead of one, they create duality. Their unity creates and maintains a balance between the opposite aspects. But why is it these two instead of another pair? The answer, and the Lovers' deeper meaning is about choice. Each choice is a duality, and throwing the balance towards one answer or another creates the life we lead. All these meanings come together to bring a message of choosing with love, not with fear or shame. The choices based on love of the higher Self will bring together the most harmonious elements and unite that which seems in conflict.

With the Hierophant's teachings, you have now come to the part of your Journey where the road diverges. With all the wisdom and guidance you have received so far, you are now ready to choose your own way. You choose who you love and what you believe. The choice may not always be easy, but your honest love will be your guide from now on. Remember the wisdom that was imparted to you before and you will stay true to your higher path.

Meanings: Unity, in its purest sense, and choices. If this card is drawn to indicate a romance, it means a relationship that has a deep soul connection. In other contexts, it means that separate parts are coming together or that a choice needs to be made. Can also indicate promises, loyalty, and oaths.

Shadow Aspect: The Lovers can mean the agony of separation. The elements at work battle each other and see-saw in confusion and pain. The balance is wildly skewed. Work on bringing things together rather then letting them swing around each other. Assess your choices more carefully.

VII – The Chariot

Astrological Association: Cancer
Kabbalah Path: Cheth, the Fence

The Chariot shows triumph in its most exuberant form. He is the conquest of the external realm.

The Chariot exerts his will over all in his path. By focusing his mind, he drives forward to meet the challenges waiting outside himself. He rushes forward and seeks to dominate in the name of further understanding. He wants to know all the answers to his questions and to accomplish the goals he has in his heart. With all this focus on the external, the High Priestess speaking from within cannot be heard. He has contemplated enough. He knows where he has come from and where he desires to go. He has eyes only for the road ahead. He is the time for action.

Having chosen your path, the Chariot comes along and sweeps you off your feet. *What are you waiting for?* is his cry as he charges forward. Now that you know where you want to go on your Journey, take on the challenges ahead with your head held high. There's a whole world out there to conquer.

Meanings: With a goal in mind or a project at hand, the Chariot arrives to encourage you to move forward with all speed. The road to success may not be easy, but with determination, there is no reason you can't achieve what you set out to do. Have confidence and take action. It can also indicate travel.

Shadow Aspect: Without the inner guidance of intuition, it is easy for the Chariot to veer off course quickly. The Chariot's power lies in his confidence, of knowing where he stands and what he's fighting for. In the shadow aspect, this becomes will with no direction, energy with no focus. You must act with an understanding of why you are moving forward. Slow down long enough to read the signs—you may not be headed where you meant to go.

VIII – Strength
Astrological Association: Leo
Kabbalah Path: Teth, the Serpent

The Chariot shows the strength in dominion, of overcoming the outer world. Strength in and of itself, though—that is the fortitude of the human spirit.

Strength turns herself inward, focusing on the exertion of will over the self rather than the world outside. Indeed, she shows not only the presentation of strength but the joy of that strength. She recognizes the passions within and dominates them, both to subdue and release as she allows. She is personal power, the will of the Self ecstatic in its own authority as it aligns with its higher purpose. For this reason, it is one of the most potent cards in the tarot and carries the force to negate all negativity around it.

On your Journey, there will be times when you will wonder if you can endure any further. Strength will arise within you to bring you back to your feet and force you to continue. No matter how many kingdoms you conquer or trophies you hang on your wall, true Strength resides within. Will over the Self is the greatest prize of all.

Meanings: Stamina and confidence in purpose. No matter how burnt-out you feel, know there is still heart within you to persevere. Recognize that will within and revel in it. Only you can give it to yourself, and only you can take it away. This is an essential element of personal power.

Shadow Aspect: Personal power only means anything if it has self-control. It takes Strength to pick your battles and not let raw emotions get the better of you. Allow them to flow when the time is right and keep them under wraps when they would only bring harm. Tame what is wild and you will come to truly understand the patience and fortitude you have within you.

IX – The Hermit
Astrological Association: Virgo
Kabbalah Path: Yod, the Open Hand

The Hermit illuminates the path on which he walks. He is the wise man who does not desire to conquer but instead holds the light of Truth, knowing that even in the darkest times, this light will guide him more than sheer willpower ever could.

While the Hermit is a model of wisdom and experience, his true meaning relates more to attainment. He is the fertility of understanding Truth. He is sometimes associated with isolation, but it should be explained that he is not withdrawn because of abhorrence to humanity or to keep Truth from others, but rather because attaining this knowledge often leads down a solitary path. The Divine Mysteries, by their very nature, place themselves where it is difficult to reach them. But not impossible. The very existence of the Hermit proves that. He sought them out, and so too can anyone.

The Journey leads you down a winding road. You may find yourself alone at times, but in the distance, the Hermit holds up the light of Truth to guide your way. But it is your inner guidance alone which compels you to reach it—the Hermit will not bring it to you. Once attained, it will reveal the fertile ground of a whole new level of spiritual ascension, and your Journey will continue.

Meanings: The Hermit speaks of the introspection of self-discovery. This can mean literally withdrawing from social life, but it can also refer to simply not allowing the outside world to distract you and instead of learning to heed your own inner light. The Hermit is a pivotal point where your current path may not mean much to you anymore. No one but yourself can guide you to the next step. Contemplate, and seek your Truth.

Shadow Aspect: The Hermit, at his worst, represents unmerited isolation. Spiritual growth does not require cutting off the world completely. You do that, and you deny others the chance to find Truth for themselves because you have hidden your light from them. Everyone has the ability to redeem themselves and seek a higher purpose. Though we may walk the path to Truth alone, we expand the light of it by helping others to seek it too.

X – The Wheel of Fortune

Astrological Association: Jupiter
Kabbalah Path: Kaph, the Palm

The Wheel of Fortune is the state of constant change. What goes up must come down, and what goes around comes around.

The Wheel circulates the fortunes of everyone, sometimes bestowing good, sometimes bad, but always with the understanding that all will change in time. This can be good news when things seem terrible and you're stuck in a rut. If fortune seems to be favoring you now, though, keep in mind that the good times can't last forever. The Wheel exemplifies the hermetic principle of rhythm. A pendulum swings both ways. Things can't stay the same, and that's okay. That is the universe at work. Just know that in time, the Wheel will swing right back around, and around, and around. In all this change, though, there is a stability to the Wheel's turning, a providence around which all fortunes happen. The center of the Wheel is Divine Intent and the understanding that all things happen for a reason. The Wheel will take you where you need to be when you need to be there. It is within this framework that our free will lies.

Your Journey takes you past the realms of the mundane. Now you enter where the great cosmic forces rule, and for the first time, with the light of Truth, you can finally begin to see them at work. The Wheel of Fortune eternally cycles overhead, revolving with the sun and the moon, the change of the seasons, the rotation of the stars through the year. From here on, you walk your Journey with the clarity of that rhythm.

Meanings: As the Wheel swings, you need to grab hold and go with its flow. Adapt to the change it heralds, for worse or for better, and take advantage of where it leads. Paths open and close throughout your life, sometimes unexpectedly, but always as an opportunity to go in a new direction.

Shadow Aspect: The Wheel is a force greater than yourself. It moves beyond your influence, and nothing you can do will stop it. If you try, it will grind you down and force you into its rhythm anyway. Stop fighting against it. Instead, learn the wisdom to work within its system.

CHAPTER 4
Major Arcana, Justice – The World

With the second half of the Major Arcana, we enter into the Cosmic Realm. Here, our Journey brings us face to face with the concepts that rule over our lives, forces so big we don't even see them from our limited perspective.

By learning control over the Self through the Mundane Realm, now when we peel back the curtain and see the greater powers, we are more able to assess our place within them. We cannot change how the universe works—we are only able to change our actions within it. But we are a part of the universe, a reflection of it, a spiritual being eternally connected to the greater picture. These figures in the Cosmic Realm exist within us as well. By recognizing how they rule our lives, we can, in turn, rule them within ourselves, and come to a greater understanding of our Selves as a whole being. Through this part of the Journey, we must put aside the ego and dive deeper still.

XI – Justice
Astrological Association: Libra
Kabbalah Path: Lamed, the Ox Goad

Justice, despite her name, does not personify what is just in the usual sense of the term. There are no ethical arguments to confuse the issue before her. Justice of the tarot is Karmic Law, and she does not care for moral debate.

In some circles, Justice is thought to be the feminine counterpart to the Fool. The Fool is zero, everything reduced to its essential potential—Justice is the system which rigorously balances everything to this potential, like a mathematical equation. The consequence is doled out to maintain equilibrium, and that equilibrium is not determined by excuses. Every action has a reaction. That is the Law. Her calculations bring about constant adjustment and satisfy all possibilities. Unlike the Wheel of Fortune, which turns regardless of us and will always circle back around, Justice deals in absolutes. Once she brings her sword down, there is no going back. There is no argument to make, for her word is completely grounded by what is fair, whether you like it or not.

Your Journey brings you to the feet of Justice. She will hold you accountable for your actions thus far. Karmic Law must be upheld before you can continue, and while she will not judge you to be good or bad, she will bring you to face the consequences of your choices. Heed her well, and understand her absolute hand. This will enable you to make wiser, more well-considered decisions as you move forward.

Meanings: Justice calls you for judgment. Usually, this is not a pleasant experience. It is difficult to face the consequences. However, this can bring a sense of relief. Once Justice has been served, you can move on without the weight of your past. Face the music so you can move on. She can also indicate a literal court case, often with a positive outcome.

Shadow Aspect: If you try to blame your mistakes on others or refuse to own up to the fact that where you are is due to what you have done, you only hinder yourself. Justice has already cast judgment on you. It is up to you to accept the ruling and gain a broader perspective. Otherwise, you will remain stuck with karmic weight.

XII – The Hanged Man
Alchemical Association: Elemental Water
Kabbalah Path: Mem, the Water

The Hanged Man is an extremely complex card and of particular significance to esoteric mystics. He shows the spiritual function of the act of baptism and sacrifice. An older name for him was 'The Drowned Man,' which highlighted this meaning and his ties to water more clearly.

The Hanged Man is submission to the divine will. His is connected to old myths regarding journeys into the underworld, most notably Orpheus, from Greek myth, and Odin from the Norse, whose story of dangling upside-down in a tree for nine days in order to enter the underworld is what influences the imagery on this card. The Hanged Man dangles upside down by one ankle, placing himself at the mercy of suffering so that he may be initiated to secret wisdom. Like baptism, it is a symbolic death of the old Self so a truer perspective may be learned. The Hanged Man is linked to water as a symbol of the underworld. He senses there is something missing and suspends himself close to death to find it. By crossing that barrier, he gains insight to the relation of the divine to the universe and resurrects to bring that knowledge back to the world, just as Odin brought back the runes when he returned.

Who you were on your Journey must be sacrificed to what you will become. The Hanged Man sets the example for you, but it is not he who can hand you the rope. You must submit by your own hand so you may enter into the realms of the unknown. Your will for the divine's—that is the exchange for greater knowledge.

Meanings: In the basic meanings derived for divination, this card usually indicates surrender. The Hanged Man tells you to release previous perspectives for they no longer serve you. Submit to the process willingly. This pause in your life is necessary.

Shadow Aspect: The Hanged Man also displays the pain of suspension. You may not want this new perspective but now you're stuck feeling strung up. Sometimes, not moving at all is the best course of action. Frustration won't fix the situation and more force will not help you.

XIII – Death

Astrological Association: Scorpio
Kabbalah Path: Nun, the Fish

This is the card of ultimate transformation. It does not describe what came before or what will come after, it only embodies the process of one becoming the other.

In the previous card of the Hanged Man, death was used symbolically as a means of insight. The Hanged Man baptizes himself in the waters of death, hangs from the tree in a gesture of death, but all with the intent of returning to himself with further knowledge gained. In the Death card, there is no returning. It is the door from one stage to the next, and whoever crosses it will not come back. The finality of Death is what makes it so scary. However, this card does not usually prophesize doom and gloom. It is very rare for it to show a literal death. Rather, it is the harbinger of change. Everything that will be razed to the ground to make room for what will be. If everything stayed the same, there would be no room for anything new. So Death brings with it a message of painful passage into a new phase of life.

On the Journey's path, a dark figure stands in the way. There is no going around—with Death, you either turn back or you submit yourself to his scythe. There is no returning to what you once were on this Journey. Despite your fear, with the knowledge gained from the sacrifice of the Hanged Man, you know the value in allowing change to happen. You cannot continue forward without it. And so you kneel before Death, and he cuts you down.

Meanings: Renewal is Death's most significant promise. Like a forest after a fire, there is now an opportunity for new growth to rise from the ashes of the old that would have smothered it. There is a purification in the process of purging what no longer serves you.

Shadow Aspect: Life has become a swamp of decay. Things have stagnated and begun to putrefy. There is clinging to the old ways, and with no flush of water to clean things out, life itself has become sick.

XIV – Temperance
Astrological Association: Sagittarius
Kabbalah Path: Samekh, the Staff

Temperance brings to mind balance, but the card is not just about balance in an of itself like it is with Justice. Temperance is the art of creating that balance.

This card is also known in some decks as Alchemy or Art. This brings to light that the balance here is sought through the synthesis of things. It can be directly connected back to the idea started in the Lovers, which talked about separate parts balancing to create a stable working relationship. In Temperance, these separate parts are instead united, and balance is created not by weighing one thing against another but by allowing them to chemically react and combine into something which is balanced in and of itself. That act is a form of creation, but rather than springing from the ground, it is the creativity of is taking what already exists and reforming it. Separate, these elements are chaotic. When fused together, they form a cohesive whole.

On your Journey, you wake from Death and find yourself changed. All the pieces of you from your Journey up to now lay scattered on the ground. The love of the Empress. The passion of the Chariot. The wisdom of the Hermit. All of them are a part of you but have not come together to form who you are. Temperance comes and gathers them and mixes them before your eyes. All you have gone through has tempered to a whole. You know where you have come from—now, pieced back together, you know where you must go from here.

Meanings: By accommodating the different parts of yourself and of your life, you strike a balance. You have become very certain in who you are and so are able to deal with what comes your way with patience and clarity. You create order out of chaos. On a more mundane level, it can indicate moderation.

Shadow Aspect: There is a sense of excess in this card. If balance needed to be created, then something was off in the first place. There is also the possibility that some things just can't be harmonized.

XV – The Devil
Astrological Association: Capricorn
Kabbalah Path: Ayin, the Eye

The Devil shows a carelessness of results. In a way, he shows the ecstasy in all material things, but also how far they can drag us down.

There is a simple joy in indulging the desires, of cutting loose and letting wild. On its surface, there is nothing wrong with that. The problem with the Devil is that he is indiscriminate in what he indulges in. He revels in it all, be it healthy or poison, and does not suffer from a moral dilemma. He does not care what is right or wrong, only what makes him feel good. The Devil tempts with his simple joy, and when you're not looking, binds you to worldly pleasures he offers. He shows the short-sighted view of pursuing what you want without regarding the consequences. He also shows the abandonment of the spiritual. One does not need to be an ascetic to fulfill their spirit, but the Devil's trap is an easy one to fall into, and if not careful, the worldly can replace the spiritual very quickly.

The Devil comes and offers you a drink. "It's a long Journey, you should take a break and have fun for a while," he says. You join him, and one drink turns into another, then another, then another, for many days. It feels so good and easy at the time. But one night you pass out, and when you wake up, you find a chained shackle around your ankle. The Devil stands over you, chain in hand. "You've done so much already. Do you really need to keep struggling? You should just stay here," he says, offers you another drink.

Meanings: Instant gratification is the Devil's mantra. This is you giving over to your shadow side and allowing bad decisions to rule your life. You are stuck in the rut of the patterns of your behavior. At his worst, he often shows addiction or abuse, even violence. His appearance in a reading shows the chains that bind you from living as your best self. However, in seeing the chains, you are that much closer to freeing yourself of them.

Shadow Aspect: The Devil has fully blinded you. Under his influence, you have grown weak and allowed your petty desires to fully own you. As a result, you suffer the consequences.

XVI – The Tower
Astrological Association: Mars
Kabbalah Path: Peh, the Mouth

More than the Death card, this is the sign that makes a tarot reader sweat. The Tower is a swift catastrophe. In this card, everything is annihilated.

The Tower is that which shakes your fundamental understanding of the universe. All the rules you have lived by thus far are shown to be lies and you are left without a leg to stand on. More than at any other time, you are left disoriented. How can you be sure of what to rely on when everything can come crashing down at a moment's notice? As painful as if may be, this is the quintessential core of spiritual awakening. It is similar to concepts from Eastern philosophy, in which Nothingness is perfection, and so all manifestations of this world, for good or evil, are blights upon Nothingness. The Tower, then, becomes the vehicle of emancipation from the existence that traps us. Its destruction shows you how foolish it was to cling to it in the first place. Life is all an illusion. Not even your ego means anything. The Tower strips you of everything so that you may see nothing within everything.

The Devil has you imprisoned in a Tower. He binds you there by placating you with an easy life and tells you how wise you are. So you stay. Every once in a while, you think about your Journey and see the path of it from your window, but always you turn back to the comfort of the Tower. The Journey was difficult, and you learned enough. Life here is good. Then, lightning strikes. In a rain of fire, it comes crumbling down, and the only way to save yourself is to leap from the window. You land on your Journey's path and watch as everything in which you found solace is destroyed. At that moment, you realize that all that matters is being present in the moment.

Meanings: This card heralds imminent calamity. Utter ruin is foreseen, and the misery of having to pick up the pieces. The confusion will destabilize everything you've ever known.

Shadow Aspect: This card is one in which the shadow aspect actually brings out the good in it. In this case, this means spiritual enlightenment. You've seen the chaos around you and used it as a means of personal growth. You now see the facade and become aware of the true value in things.

XVII – The Star
Astrological Association: Aquarius
Kabbalah Path: Tzaddi, the Fish Hook

After the apocalypse of the Tower, in the light of the Star, we see the Truth revealed in its full light. She is the gifts of the Spirit flowing freely.

The Star brings immortality in that there is no separation between the core of the Self and the Divine Spirit. She embodies the personal growth that happens after the Tower. This is the soul who withstood the worst and came out its best. This is because, with the Star, all things are fully understood and appreciated for what they are, be they good or evil. Everything has a purpose in this world. In her light, blessings flow forth, and the farthest Star is within reach.

Through the razing of the Tower, your Journey has stripped of all that kept you from what you are at the center of your being. The ego has been dissolved and you exist in your purest sense. The Star shines down on you and pours the Divine down onto you like water. Faith is your power.

Meanings: Its most basic interpretation is hope in the sense that the Star shows bright prospects. That's only a surface reading, though. The Star represents much more. The Divine is everywhere, and you are connected to it. One does not need hope when united fully and totally to Spirit. Remain open to the gifts pouring down on you.

Shadow Aspect: There's an arrogance here, an attitude of being higher-than-thou. This is not true spiritual inspiration. If your faith is tested, you may find it to be shaken easily until the Star can shine through for real.

XVIII – The Moon
Astrological Association: Pisces
Kabbalah Path: Koph, the Mind

This is the dark night of the soul. After the enlightenment found in the Star, after that blissful, perfect fulfillment, the soul swings back into doubt and fear. This is the power of the Moon.

This is a time when it will feel like you're feeling your way through the dark. The Moon is the unknown. This kind of pressure raises the animal instinct in all of us and so the natural response of fear. This is all subconscious activity of the deep processes that drive us. In defense of the intensity of the previous two cards, the subconscious draws up veils again and makes us see bogeymen where there are only shadows. Now, more than ever, our intuition is our only guide.

The brightness of the Star fades, and you are only left with the light of the Moon on your Journey. You stumble and fall, and freeze in fear. Everywhere around you, danger lurks and wolves howl. You don't know how you will ever make it through. But deep within you, something pushes you along, makes you look twice at the shadows. You begin to see they are just branches moving in the wind, and that the wolves are just dogs alert to your presence. Uneasily, you move through your fear and push forward through the night.

Meanings: This card serves to show you that there may be many things hidden deep within your psyche that are rearing their head. You may not know what they are exactly, but they are affecting you, and you feel their presence. This card embodies uncertainty and fear. Things are never what they seem under the light of the Moon.

Shadow Aspect: This is the silence when you know there should be sound. There is still an element of fear, but this silence only brings out what is unknown. You know there are intuitive messages coming your way, but you can't hear them. And yet, you're still afraid, because you know there's something out there you need to be aware of. Be still and listen harder.

XIX – The Sun

Astrological Association: The Sun
Kabbalah Path: Resh, the Head

The Sun exposes all visions for what they are and detangles all mysteries. It is the most positive card in the deck and shines its light on everything around it.

Rather than the subconscious rising up, this is complete consciousness. This is the soul in full realization of itself. There is a certain simplicity in this card, of just being what it is, the warmth and joy and energy of all happiness made manifest. The subconscious and the conscious are joined as one. The soul goes forth as a whole being.

After the night comes the dawn. The Sun rises over the horizon, chasing away all shadows and leaving the Journey clear for you ahead. You bask in its light, allow the warmth to charge you, and with a deep breath, continue on your path in its light.

Meanings: This is a time when you can share the absolute best of yourself. This card has a lot of energy in it and may indicate a period where you will be so full to brim you won't know what to do with yourself. Life is good with this card. If you're looking for a 'yes' in your reading, this is a 'yes' shouted from the mountaintops.

Shadow Aspect: Everything is exposed in the light of the Sun. Some things may come to light that may not be pleasant to look at. However, the Sun is a uniformly positive card, even in negative contexts, so this exposure is always a good thing, like hanging something out in the sun to air out. Nothing can ruin this beautiful day.

XX – Judgment
Alchemical Association: Fire
Kabbalah Path: Shin, the Tooth

It is time for the last transition. This is the phase beyond change and beyond death. This is eternal life waiting if the call will be answered.

This card was originally called 'The Last Judgment,' referring to the Christian Book of Revelations in which the end of the world is on the horizon, and the dead rise from their graves to face the end of times. In the tarot, it symbolizes the soul aligning with its highest purpose. The call has been issued, and the enlightened rise and leave their worldliness behind, as the spirit leaves the body in death. It may sound a bit morbid, but in actuality, this is the greatest aspiration the spirit can have. In Eastern terminology, this is the receiving of Nirvana.

The Journey leads to you a gravesite, open and empty. It is your size, and you know it is yours. Overhead, you hear a trumpet. The clouds part and the angel of Judgment descends to you and offers you a hand. "You have completed your Journey," the angel says. "Come and fulfill your true purpose in this life." Taking the angel's hand, you rise into the sky.

Meanings: This card shows entering into a significant phase of your life. You may have come to a major crossroads where you have two distinct choices: go the safe way and stay where you are, or heed the call and go in the unknown desires of your heart. Your purpose in this life may take many twists and turns to get to, but with every twist and turn that brings you closer to it, Judgment will be there to remind you that you are on the way.

Shadow Aspect: The soul is willing, but the flesh is weak. You hear the call, but whether out of fear or a sense of comfort, you do not listen. Instead of growing, you stay where you are. In some readings, this card also shows up to refer to legal issues, usually indicating a sentence will be passed.

XXI – The World
Alchemical Association: Earth
Kabbalah Path: Tav, the Mark

The World is a card of celebration. It is the Cosmic Joke, of the pure and utter belly-laugh bliss that comes when you attain enlightenment and realize that you are what you are seeking.

Here, as in the Fool, the World is the paradox of being the end and the beginning. The World and the Fool are one and the same but also opposites. The Fool heads out from nothing, and the World returns to nothing. They form a complete cycle. Manifestation has culminated to the highest degree, and with that process done, seeks to return to zero and begin anew. For that is the cycle of the universe and all things within it, which has been reflected many times throughout the Major Arcana. Endings create beginnings, and beginnings create endings. The ending shown in the World is the most perfect and bright. The great work of the soul has come to an end with the soul joining with the universe. By doing so, it becomes nothingness once again, and so starts anew.

Having passed through Judgment, you arrive at the end of your Journey. You now recognize that all the challenges you went through on the way were there to prime you for this. You are the universe, and you always were. It only now, though, that you see this for what it is. So you meld into the nothingness, complete and whole within yourself and so complete and whole with the World. You know you will manifest again as the Fool, ready to start again, but for now, you enter bliss.

Meanings: This is a sign of change manifesting. One phase of your life is complete, so prepare to begin another. With this comes a sense of closure, and the joy of having accomplished so much, but also excitement at what is to come. Take the lessons learned from this stage of your life and use it to help you with the next. In a more grounded sense, the World can also indicate the literal globe, possibly travel abroad.

Shadow Aspect: You can't move forward. There is a nagging sense of being incomplete, and so you remain immobile in life, allowing inertia to dictate your life. Do not let the fear of challenges to hold you back—they are there to help you grow.

CHAPTER 5
Minor Arcana, The Pips

Having gone through the lofty ideas of the Fool's Journey, we come to the Minor Arcana. While the Major Arcana explores the archetypes of universal influence, these cards deal with the aspects of our everyday lives. Their meaning may pertain to more mundane things, but because of that, they also tend to be much more specific and relatable. In this chapter, we will be exploring the pip cards, which are the numbers of the suits Ace through Ten.

There are four suits of the Minor Arcana: Wands, Cups, Swords, and Pentacles. Following the philosophy of alchemy, these are the four elements that combine to create the world we live in. They are the basic onto themselves, but it is in the synthesis of these that we are created as spiritual beings.

Wands are the element of fire. They are a masculine, active property that relates to the spirit. They are the creative will, initiative, and passion. The cards in this suit often speak of pursuing goals.

Cups are water, a feminine, passive element. This suit displays the depths of our emotions. They are love, relationships of all kinds, and our dreams and fantasies.

Swords relate to air. The dourest of the suits, it has a masculine, active personality and has to do with the pain of the mind. It is thought, strife, conflict, and communication, especially as it deals with logic and truth.

Pentacles, sometimes called Coins, is the earth element. It is feminine and passive and often indicates money. More symbolically, it is the body. It is our material sensations. Endurance, patience, and practicality are the theme of this suit, and one of a slow, steady approach.

To explore the pips, rather than going through each suit individually from Ace to Ten, we're going to use the framework of numerology, the study of the mystical relationships of numbers. In regards to our subject, numerology has ancient connections to the Kabbalah and alchemy, and so was used alongside those to determine the meanings of the cards.

In this chapter, the four suits will be broken down into the numbers, discussing each set of four cards as the numerology applies to the suit's characteristics. The Kabbalah placement of each set of numbers on the Tree of Life will be noted at the top of the page. Each card has a title that is a one or two word summation of what the card boils down to. Astrological significance will be listed with the card's meaning and shadow aspect.

As with the Major Arcana, the astrological and Kabbalic information is more for future reference if you choose to delve deeper into hermetic associations. While doing so can help you unlock deeper meanings into the cards, for now, while you're learning, it will not impact your ability to read the cards.

Aces – *Kether, the Source*

Aces are the quintessence for each of their suits. They are each element in their purest spiritual sense, signified by the fact that even in decks with illustrated pip cars, the Aces usually do not have a figure on the card. They are energy unmanifested, limitless in their potential but without form or shape themselves. When they show up in a reading, they are an offering of what could be, if you take what they have to offer and realize something concrete with it. All Aces can indicate pregnancy or birth.

Ace of Wands: The Root of Fire. Aries, Leo, Sagittarius. This is the motivation of inspiration. This is the card that tells you to follow your passions. If you have a new idea, this is your cue to go for it. In the shadow aspect, a burst of energy with no direction.

Ace of Cups: The Root of Water. Cancer, Scorpio, Pisces. An open heart overflowing with love. Your subconscious is a vessel for spiritual joy and now you can't help but show it. Let your imagination unfurl and pursue something creative. It is the expression of self-love that permeates into everything around you. In the shadow aspect, this is a false love that damages. This can mean either yourself or someone taking advantage of you.

Ace of Swords: The Root of Air. Gemini, Aquarius, Libra. This is the Sword of Truth. With it comes complete clarity of thought. It is a powerful card, showing triumph in understanding. It is also the energy of learning something new. In the shadow aspect, this indicates misguided judgment. You've made a call without the full truth, leading to disaster.

Ace of Pentacles: The Root of Earth. Capricorn, Taurus, Virgo. This is pure abundance. While it can indicate wealth coming, more often it means manifestation of material things that will aid you. It is your desires turning real. In the shadow aspect, this shows the evil of wealth. You might be getting what you want, but it is not what you need, and it will fail to truly enrich you.

Twos – *Chokmah, the Wisdom*
In numerology, two is the number of dualities. With this is also the sense of balance needed to keep the dual aspects stable. So within the tarot, twos often show up to point out choices that need to be made, or partnerships.

Two of Wands: Dominion. Mars in Aries. This is discovery, risks, and developing a plan. In the energy of fire, the duality of this card suggests weighing the risks of staying where you are or taking a chance. In shadow aspect, it is fear of surprise. It can also mean wishful thinking.

Two of Cups: Love. Venus in Cancer. In water, the energy of two becomes one of loving connections. The card is the most positive sign in reading on romance. It can also show relationships of friendship and family. This is synergy and sympathy at its greatest level. In shadow aspect, this translates to clinginess or co-dependence.

Two of Swords: Peace Restored, Inner Balance. Moon in Libra. This is the uneasy harmony of a stalemate. Despite the positive connotations of words like 'peace' and 'balance' in Sword energy, this becomes tense conformity. It is refusing to make a decision so as not to rock the boat. In shadow aspect, this becomes outright duplicity, of using falsehood to take the easy way rather than do the work facing a decision would bring.

Two of Pentacles: Change, Balance. Jupiter in Capricorn. In practical Pentacles, the earth energy in the number two creates a juggling act. It is the balance of all the things you must deal with in day-to-day life. It is work and play, pain and pleasure, duty and rest. All these elements are in balance and you are in control of them, despite any trouble that may try to disrupt your concentration. In shadow aspect, the balls have dropped. You're trying to keep a good face, but underneath there is a sense of panic you may not be able to keep up, and the stress is setting in.

Threes – *Binah, the Knowledge*
Threes are the manifestation of growth. They are groups congregating for a purpose. They fuel creative endeavors, and so represent energy moving forward. If ace was the self, and two were individuals coming together, then three is their unity creating something more, like how couples come together to make a family.

Three of Wands: Virtue, Established Strength. Sun in Aries. This card is progress, of taking established plans and building them into a working system. Dare to dream bigger. It can also signify business endeavors or travel. In shadow aspect, it is avoiding challenges and staying within current limitations. Can also be disappointment with the way things are going.

Three of Cups: Abundance, Joy. Mercury in Cancer. It is happiness in the community and having a good time. You are surrounded by people who wish to celebrate with you, to help you, to lift you up as you lift them up. In shadow aspect, it is an overindulgence in your social life, perhaps drinking too much or spending too much time with friends rather than on your daily obligations. There is also an element of gossip.

Three of Swords: Sorrow. Saturn in Libra. Another name for this is the heartbreak card. This is deep hurt and grief, and in this sense, it is an emotional release as your mind processes the pain. In shadow aspect, rather than processing sadness, you dwell on it, and the mental alienation creates negative self-talk and confusion.

Three of Pentacles: Works. Mars in Capricorn. This is teamwork at its best. Plans have come together, everyone has been assigned their tasks, and the collaboration of craft and skill is at its creative peak. You are on the right track. In shadow aspect, this card is mediocrity. Either the work put into a project isn't at its best, or the project itself does not allow for the best to shine through. May also show that the work is not taken seriously by those involved.

Fours – *Chesed, the Empathy*
Like the four corners of a square, four represents stability and form. Things have materialized and developed structure. No longer is the energy just an idea in development, but now a solid reality.

Four of Wands: Completion, Abundance. Venus in Aries. This is the card of the home. With the fiery energy of the Wands settled, it shows how far you've come and all the things you've accomplished. It is a time for celebration and recognizing all you have. Because this card is so positive, it has no shadow aspect. It only serves to emphasize how much beauty and prosperity there is in your life.

Four of Cups: Luxury, Blended Pleasure. Moon in Cancer. This card is about having so much that you can't, or won't, accept anything else. There is a sense of discontent here, of being spoiled for choice. The stability of four in watery energy turns into dissatisfaction and boredom. In shadow aspect, there is so much disillusionment so you may not notice when something genuinely amazing enters your life.

Four of Swords: Truce, Rest. Jupiter in Libra. The retreat is indicated when this card shows up. This is the time for recovery. Seclusion is needed to heal up before marching out to battle again. Some readers see this as a card of illness and death. In shadow aspect, this is deliberate avoidance, of hunkering down when it's time for action.

Four of Pentacles: Power. Sun in Capricorn. This is securing accumulated resources. Frugality is needed, and keeping a close eye on what is coming in or being spent. In shadow aspect, this degrades to hoarding and opposing anything that might change the status quo.

Fives – *Gevurah, the Judgment*
Five is the number that disrupts the firm stability of the previous fours. Because stability feels right and safe, the appearance of this disruption brings stress over the changes it instigates. However, it is a natural progression, and should not be considered necessarily a bad thing.

Five of Wands: Strife. Saturn in Leo. This signifies competition. In a sense, it's like entry into a tournament where you must brandish your skills to come out on top. Everyone wants to win, but there is no real vitriol between the players. In shadow aspect, this competition turns into a fight and becomes a personal war. With everyone fighting so hard to be heard, it only leads to disruption with no resolution in sight.

Five of Cups: Disappointment, Pleasure Lost. Mars in Scorpio. Because of the emotional quality of the Cups, the strife of five becomes the shock of loss. Things didn't meet your expectations, and so you grieve what could have been. In shadow aspect, this furthers into a dwelling in guilt and regret.

Five of Swords: Defeat. Venus in Aquarius. Rather than a fair fight like in the Five of Wands, here there is destruction for the sake of destruction. This is the card of bad blood. If it shows up in questions of litigation, it's to say that some fights are not worth having. This card is so negative, there is very little positive to say about it, and so becomes its own shadow aspect. Its only advice is to pick your battles.

Five of Pentacles: Worry, Trouble. Mercury in Taurus. This is material hardship, usually a harbinger of financial difficulties. It is the destitution feared by the hoarder from the Four of Pentacles. How well you can make it through this time depends on your ability to bring all that you have left and piece it back together. In shadow aspect, this loss descends into a chaos that will waste what resources you have.

Sixes – *Tiferet, the Beauty*

Sixes are the energy of harmony. While maybe not as steady as Four, all elements are nevertheless balanced after the schism of the Fives. Sixes rule cooperation and communication and have the energy in them to adapt to possible difficulties in the future.

Six of Wands: Victory. Jupiter in Leo. This is great news coming in and triumph over adversity. This is an important milestone that shows your persistence has been rewarded. You are recognized for your ability to overcome challenges. In shadow aspect, there is fear of someone else's victory and the treachery of arrogance.

Six of Cups: Pleasure, Friendship. Sun in Scorpio. This shows harmony in all your relationships. There is fun and freedom in this card and usually depicted with children. This is often called the card of nostalgia and is often read as the past coming back into play, or pleasure in memories. Either way, it is an extremely positive card in a reading. In shadow aspect, rather than exposing some negative quality, this card turns its positivity towards the future and may indicate a renewal of some sort.

Six of Swords: Science, Earned Success. Mercury in Aquarius. In the Thoth deck, this card is called 'Science' because it represents intelligence not divided but brought together to attain its goals. In most other decks, this concept is illustrated as the focus of the mind to bring itself out of troubled waters. It's usually presented as a card of transition, but does not necessarily carry that meaning at all times. In shadow aspect, it is simply these intellectual elements not being harmonized.

Six of Pentacles: Success. Moon in Taurus. To some readers, it is the card of loans and debts. Inherent in this message, though, is the complex interplay of giving and receiving. On the surface, this card speaks of the security and means to give to others and the gratification that comes from charity. On the other hand, it also brings up the act of receiving. One cannot give to one who does not want to receive. In many instances, favors are given in the expectation that something will be given back later, and so receiving is not as passive as taking from the open hand. This relationship is not a mere hierarchy but an exchange. In shadow aspect, it shows the greediness in this relationship at its worst. The giver may be reluctant to share even though they have more than enough. The receiver may beg for more with no intention of paying back or with any mind towards the giver's resources. Thus, the exchange crumbles.

Sevens – *Netzah, the Endurance*
Harmony has been unbalanced, and so once again, each suit must go through a period of discomfort. However, the Sevens carry with them a sense of assessment the Fives did not. Through knowledge attained, each suit has more ability to reflect on their struggles and deal with them appropriately.

Seven of Wands: Valour, Courage. Mars in Leo. This is a card of struggle, but of one where you have the vantage position. You are a rising star, reaching the top of your field, and others are clamoring to take you down or compete with you for what you have. This often shows a situation where you must negotiate and compromise in order to be successful. In shadow aspects, this pressure is causing anxiety, which only makes you vulnerable. Though you have the advantage, you are on the back foot.

Seven of Cups: Debauch, Illusory Success. Venus in Scorpio. The illusion of fantasy distracts you in this card. You dream of so many ideas that it's unrealistic to dwell on all of them, and yet dwell you do, indulging the fantasy rather than working to make it real. This is one card in which the shadow aspect is actually an improvement, suggesting the focus of your will on one choice and showing determination to make it come to fruition.

Seven of Swords: Futility, Shortened Force. Moon in Aquarius. This card is one of the biggest red flags in the deck. This is theft, trickery, and deception in all aspects. Plans will fail when this card is around. However, unlike the Five of Swords, this is a passive card that can be overturned easily. In a more positive connotation, it shows that some workaround may be sussed out if you look at a problem from a different perspective. In shadow aspect, it shows slander, bad advice, and secrets.

Seven of Pentacles: Failure, Unfulfilled Success. Saturn in Taurus. On one hand, this card's titles give it the meaning of a project that is draining you. You've dedicated so much effort to something, but now there are no results of your work. On another, though, this card speaks of the patience needed for the long-term view. Just because the harvest not here now doesn't mean it won't be reaped later. The difference lays in the connotation of the reading, and whether or not you're putting your efforts into the right things. In shadow aspect, this shows you lack the patience to see a project through to the end. You've thrown down the stake and have given up. Again, the connotation will reveal if that is called for or simply the result of frustration.

Eights – *Hod, the Submission*

Eights show the mastery of each suit and the capability of turning its energy into directed action. The Eights came through the imbalance of the Sevens and now work to react against it. It is through them that we can head towards true accomplishment.

Eight of Wands: Swiftness. Mercury in Sagittarius. This is an extremely dynamic card. It is pure motion, a great burst of speed towards the end of an endeavor. You are aiming straight at your goal, like an arrow flying. In shadow aspect, this energy can turn on itself and create disputes and in-fighting. There is no room for doubt at this speed.

Eight of Cups: Indolence, Abandoned Success. Saturn in Pisces. This is another card of loss, but unlike the Five of Cups, this shows a loss you choose. In the Eight of Cups, you walk away from something. In its titles, it is suggested this is due to laziness. There may be a tendency to drift from one thing to the next and always leaving things unfinished. Sometimes, though, this can indicate something in which you put a lot of emotion into only to find it wasn't nearly as important as you thought. A loss, yes, but a recognized one, and something that needs to be left behind even though it's a difficult thing to do. Another card with a positive shadow aspect, it reveals finding joy in moving on and willingly dropping the weight you've carried.

Eight of Swords: Interference, Bondage. Jupiter in Gemini. This is a card of entrapment. Deliberate sabotage may be indicated. You were placed in this situation, perhaps by circumstances outside your influence, but this is only temporary bondage. You're the only one keeping you here. The influence of the eights in airy Swords means you can take your power back. In shadow aspect, this is an unforeseen tragedy with no apparent way through.

Eight of Pentacles: Prudence. Sun in Virgo. Discipline motivates this card's energy. This is the card of the apprentice, one who toils at their work with the pure intent of gaining craftsmanship. This is skill at work and business. In shadow aspect, it is the vanity of your craft. May also be too much attention to detail to your detriment.

Nines – *Yesod, the Connection*

Nines are complete fulfillment. In some schools of thought, nine is the summit of perfection, and in the tarot, this has been attained in each suit. All struggles and accomplishments are now brought to their fullest potential.

Nine of Wands: Strength. Moon in Sagittarius. This is the energy of having come through adversity and being all the stronger for it. You have built your ground and can stand on it. It's a lot of responsibility to defend it, but you know you can take on the challenges. In shadow aspect, it indicates weariness and paranoia.

Nine of Cups: Happiness. Jupiter in Pisces. Known as the Yes card or the Wish card, this is complete satisfaction. When this shows up, everything is going your way and there's nothing to be unhappy about. In shadow aspect, something feels like it's missing from what should be a great fortune, like the emptiness in wealth.

Nine of Swords: Cruelty, Despair. Mars in Gemini. Unfortunately, since the Swords are so negative, in their culmination they bring the only desolation. This is pure anxiety, the dark thoughts that keep you up at night, and utter failure. In shadow aspect, it is still doubt and shame.

Nine of Pentacles: Gain, Wealth. Venus in Virgo. This is the result of the discipline shown in the Eight of Pentacles. You have been rewarded, and now live in comfort and luxury, able to enjoy the riches of life. This is the pinnacle of self-worth. In shadow aspect, this is bad faith in something that won't work out.

Tens – *Malkuth, the Kingdom*
Ten is the end of the cycle, and the promise of something new. In that sense, they could be considered as the period between one sentence and the next. They are completion after fulfillment and renewal.

Ten of Wands: Oppression. Saturn in Sagittarius. This card shows the weight of the many responsibilities garnered by attaining the goals you set. Any success comes with its own problems. A choice is implied here: you can either carry on, or you can drop the load. In shadow aspect, the responsibilities actually inhibit success. There is a warning here against using force for all things at all times.

Ten of Cups: Satiety, Perfected Success. Mars in Pisces. This the heart's desires completely fulfilled. This is family, romance, and friendship perfected in love. In shadow aspect, disruption of this state.

Ten of Swords: Ruin. Sun in Gemini. This is the card of ultimate pain. All things seem to be going wrong and you are defeated. Many tears will be had in this card's energy. However, being ten energy, there is a sense that it is not permanent. In shadow aspect, this energy turns positive and promises new dawn.

Ten of Pentacles: Wealth. Mercury in Virgo. Legacy is the center of this card. While the Ten of Cups shows the emotional home, the Ten of Pentacles shows family inheritance. Your goals have provided for you, and now you can provide for everyone else. In shadow aspect, rather than showing a secure fortune, there is a sense of chance here, and the possibility of loss, like putting all your money into the lottery.

CHAPTER 6
Minor Arcana, The Court Cards

Each suit is ruled by figures of royalty known as the Court cards. There is a Page, a Knight, a Queen, and a King. These can be some of the most puzzling cards to decipher as their meanings range widely and need to be contextualized within each individual reading.

They can indicate people, each one in each suit representing a certain type of personality. Sometimes they mean specifically a man or woman but can also mean someone of any gender who displays that type masculine or feminine energy. They also personify aspects of ourselves, the different attitudes we can use to resolve problems. Once you understand the character of each one, it will be easier to glean their meanings within readings.

Pages
These are the young ones of the Court cards. They are messengers and students, an expression of youthful vigor with no sense of self-awareness. They are keen to learn and bring with them the potential for new ideas or projects. In the Rider Waite-Smith, they are represented by boys, but their energy corresponds more towards the feminine so in many other decks they are girls and will be referred to as such here. They often indicate children or teenagers, but they can also show up to highlight parts of yourself that are inexperienced or a situation you don't know much about. Because of their potential for growth, they are associated with the element of Earth.

Page of Wands: Earth of Fire. She is ambitious and has a lot to prove. She is a restless catalyst, someone brimming with ideas but maybe not the patience to see a project through to the end. There is a light-heartedness to her that can be inspiring. At her worst, though, in shadow aspect, she is all theatrics without substance and acts with undeserved confidence.

Page of Cups: Earth of Water. She is the poetic mind, a sweet and gentle romantic who likes to study literature and art. She is characterized as a sensitive, amiable soul. She often brings messages of marriages, pregnancy, or a new romance. She also offers a new project, often in a creative vein. In shadow aspect, she can fall to slothfulness easily.

Page of Swords: Earth of Air. She is a firm personality, sometimes even called aggressive, but displays a discerning practicality. She is associated with spying in the sense that she accumulates information with great enthusiasm for future use. At her best, she can resolve disputes with ease of logic. In shadow aspect, she becomes vengeful and uses her gifts to pull underhanded tactics that win her no friends.

Page of Pentacles: Earth of Earth. Slow and steady is this Page's work ethic. She's a planner, someone who sets goals in mind and applies themselves carefully in order to achieve it. While she is enthusiastic, she's realistic, more interested in getting it right than in bowling everyone over. Out of all the Pages, she is the one most likely to indicate a literal student. In shadow aspect, she is inconsistent and prone to wasting her time and resources if she has no set goal to work on.

Knights

Knights are action-oriented. They represent masculine energies and young adulthood. More mature than the Pages, they nevertheless tend towards excessive behaviors, not having the experience to temper their ideologies. They are constantly on the go and signify change and movement, and therefore are connected with the element of Air.

Knight of Wands: Air of Fire. He is the courageous harbinger of change. He's impulsive and reckless but does not seek conflict for the sake of conflict. He simply wants to throw his strength into that which he believes in. He revels in taking action and can be generous in giving that energy to others who need it. If he's not careful, though, in his shadow aspect, he can turn prideful and cruel and refuse to listen if he's on the wrong side of a moral issue.

Knight of Cups: Air of Water. A charming dreamer, this is the romantic Knight ruled by his heart who uses his passions as his guide. He is an idealist, which give him the attractive quality of having a grand vision he's working towards. He often brings tidings of a relationship or an invitation. In shadow aspect, he is secretive and selfish, believing his artistic creed is more important than goodwill towards others. His ideals may be too high to reach and so he ends up distracting himself chasing dreams rather than focusing on the here and now. There's also an element of seduction.

Knight of Swords: Air of Air. The most war-like of the Knights, he's the sort to charge ahead with no regard to danger. He is intellectual and upholds the highest standards of rational thought, focused only on his ambitions. In shadow aspect, his degree of rationality can leave him without a moral compass to build his ideas on. He could readily turn an indifferent eye to the consequences of his actions, resulting in a wrathful disregard for others.

Knight of Pentacles: Air of Earth. This is the methodical, practical Knight. Though he may be slower than the others, he is extremely capable because of his competence. His cautious nature allows him to plan ahead and think through a project before moving forward. In his shadow aspect, he can become stubborn and refuse to take in any ideas which do not align with his own. His practical, grounded approach to things may make him insensitive to the emotional needs of others.

Queens
Queens are the middle age of the suits and display feminine maturity. Each rules through the experiences of coming to understand herself and others. They all nurture to some degree and usually show the different ways creativity can express itself. While not domineering, they nevertheless heavily influence those around them and garner respect for the insight they provide. Because of their emotional strength, they are associated with the element of Water.

Queen of Wands: Water of Fire. This dominant Queen wields authority with bold independence. Her creativity springs from her persistence and adaptability. She is magnetic, often controlling the conversation in a room by the force of her personality. She is the best friend anyone could ever hope for, capable of deep affection and generosity. But, in her shadow aspect, she is the worst enemy you ever gained. She can be jealous, vain, exhibit a quick temper, and has a tendency to brood.

Queen of Cups: Water of Water. She is the tranquil mother who is deeply sensitive to the emotional well-being of those she loves. Empathy and dreaminess are her most distinct qualities. She lives by her imagination and is usually highly gifted in the arts. Intuitive, she can often indicate a healer or psychic. In shadow aspect, she can be prone to sinking so deep into her psyche that she becomes confused by illusions. She may have a hard time distinguishing her emotions from those of others.

Queen of Swords: Water of Air. Highly perceptive, this Queen does not deal with insincerity from anyone. She is an intelligent and keen observer, and swift to bring her foot down if she senses immoral action. Ruled by her head, she remains at all times independent in thought and is characterized by efficient bluntness. She never allows her emotions to dictate her will. In shadow aspect, her bluntness can be cruel if her intent turns malicious. Her intellectual talents can be deceitful if she uses her quick observational skills against others.

Queen of Pentacles: Water of Earth. She exhibits the strength of quiet, hard work and greatness of heart. She is often very domestic. Through practical means, she keeps a secure budget and demonstrates a lot of common sense. She does what she can with what she has and still finds the resources to be kind to others. In her shadow aspect, she becomes mechanical, living day to day with no drive to change her lot. She can be prone to substance abuse, preferring escape rather than action to deal with drudgery.

Kings

Here, in the Kings, we see the full culmination of each suit's potential in older, masculine energy. He is the most mature, the most experienced, the most stable, the one in full control of himself and that which he rules over. He is a provider who creates stability for those around him. Because of their drive to bring things to completion, they are associated with the element of Fire.

King of Wands: Fire of Fire. A natural leader who rules with absolute honesty and nobility. He is swift to act and knows how to push people to create what he envisions. In shadow aspect, he can be fierce and cruel, even brutal, in driving towards his goals.

King of Cups: Fire of Water. Like all Cup Court cards, he embodies creativity, but his is the mind that can apply emotional intelligence to his creations. In personality, he is sensitive and passive, with a quiet authority. In shadow aspect, he is superficial and easily influenced, and prone to fall victim to his own sensual tastes.

King of Swords: Fire of Air. He is a militant king, a stern authority who wields a heavy sword of judgment. He commands harshly but with fairness, upholding the law to the best of his abilities. In shadow aspect, he acts on decision without reflection, and enforces his rule with futile violence.

King of Pentacles: Fire of Earth. To apply a legend to him, he is King Midas, metaphorically turning everything he touches into gold. He is successful in business with a good instinct for the worth of his resources and labor. He cultivates the richness of life, be that monetarily or otherwise. In shadow aspect, he lacks foresight or initiative, preoccupied with only what is in front of him. At his worst, he has an ugliness over petty matters and can be oppressive.

CHAPTER 7
Spreads

Now that we've gone over the meanings of the cards, you must bring them together in a reading. While it is entirely possible to just throw the cards down willy-nilly and get an impression from them, usually readers will place the cards down in a certain order. This order is known as a spread.

There are dozens upon dozens upon dozens of different spreads to pull from. Any search online for tarot spreads will pull up more website than you could ever sift through that offer spreads for every kind of question. For example, there are spreads specifically tailored for romance, careers, or general ones for looking at the year ahead. Unlike the tarot itself, which is so structured, spreads are very fluid and can be adapted to fit your needs.

In this book, we will cover very basic spreads to help you ease into reading, and also talk about some more distinct ones for when you're ready to try something more complicated.

It's recommended that before you dive too deep into these spreads, go ahead and read the next chapter on reading with context. Of course, you're more than welcome to give reading a shot right out the gate, but Chapter 8 might help you to understand how to piece together the cards you see in each spread.

On Shuffling
The first thing to do when doing a reading is to shuffle the cards. There is no particular method for doing this, and every reader has their own approach. Some do a riffle shuffle, some overhand. Some spread the cards out face-down and pull them from the pile. Go with whatever feels comfortable. It is also common to cut the deck before laying them out, which means setting the deck face-down, splitting it into sections, usually about three, and then reintegrating them again in a different order.

Often, the most common question when starting is, "What do I do? How do I know when to stop?" The answer is, tarot is all about intuition. Some readers will shuffle through a deck a preset number of times, while others will keep going until it feels right. If you're doing a reading for another person, known as a querent, this becomes even more variant. Some readers don't like anyone else touching their cards and will ask for the querent's question to ask the cards themselves. Others will shuffle the deck and then let the querent cut the deck. Still, others will let the querent do it all and let them either ask the question out loud or focus on it silently in their minds.

No method is wrong or right. The main thing is that you focus on your question while you shuffle. Repeat it over and over if you like, and visualize the person or situation you're asking about. This focus is important since it not only preps your mind for the reading but also helps draw the energy of the reading to that intent. Once you have done this, then you can lay out the cards.

Three-Card Spread
For our first spread, we're going to do the three-card reading. This one is simple but extremely flexible, and able to give you a quick glance into the question. Once you're done shuffling, take the top three cards off the top of the deck and lay them out in a row in the order you drew them. From here, you can begin interpreting.

The great thing about the three-card spread is its versatility. In some readings, it can be read as the first card being the past, the middle card the present, the third the future. This is very useful for establishing the context of the question. But these three cards can also be read as the querent's mind, body, and soul and relate the cards to how they're thinking, acting, and feeling. It can be situation-action-outcome. Or it can be structure-less, and you read the cards as they flow together seamlessly, forming an overall picture of the answer. This is a great spread for practice since it is so quick and will train your mind to see the story in the cards.

Nine-Card Spread
This is the natural progression of the three-card spread. It is a rectangle created by three rows of three cards, which takes the idea of the three card reading and then extrapolates it.

The nine-card spread is every bit as versatile as the three-card, but obviously, it provides a lot more information. Now you have a grid to read, and this grid can be approached a number of different ways, each giving more depth to the reading. This grid is 1-2-3, 4-5-6, 7-8-9.

The first way is to look at the rows. It's the most instinctive way to read them initially. Usually, the rows are read as 1-2-3 being the conscious, 4-5-6 our current state, and 7-8-9 as kind of the undercurrent to the reading.

The second way to read the nine-card spread is to then look at the columns. This is 1-4-7, 2-5-8, 3-6-9. This is similar to the three-card as it can be seen as past-present-and future. But when you turn the reading this way, suddenly a card that means one thing when read with the one next to it becomes different when read with the card below it.

The center card can also be taken to be the central theme of the reading. This card is what everything turns around, and the framing cards are all the various elements circling that center. This provides some interesting context for the reading.

You can also read the whole thing strung together, like the text on a page. Starting with one, go through and link all of them into one statement or story. Reading it this way is incredibly dense and may be difficult to get the hang of at first, but it's brilliant at giving an overview of the situation.

Since this spread is a block of cards, it can be read in any of these ways. Sometimes, only one way is needed. Sometimes, all the ways of looking at it jump at you. It depends on the question, and of course, what the cards are telling you.

Cross Spread
The Cross spread is not to be confused with the Celtic Cross, but it is useful in helping you build up to that. For this one, you'll make a cross shape with your cards.

The first card, which we will call 1 here, is laid down. 1 represents you, or the querent, as you stand in the situation.

To the left of it, you place 2. This is the desires or mistakes that brought you here.

Above it, place 3. This is what helps you.

Below, place 4. This is what hinders you.

And lastly, 5 is to the right. This is the outcome.

The outcome card is an important one in a lot of different spreads. Sometimes, it's separate from a different immediate future card, such as in the Celtic Cross. The difference is the length of time. The outcome card often refers to how a situation will ultimately conclude, and this can be far down the line. Tarot has no sense of time the way we do, so to it, something two years away is the same as something two days ahead. So the outcome is the final conclusion, what we can anticipate from our actions as the situation resolves, whenever that may be.

Sometimes, outcome cards vastly contradict the rest of the reading. You'll be going along with a beautiful, rosy reading, and then pull the outcome card and find it to be a jarring omen. Or, in contrast, sometimes a reading looks really, really bad, and then the outcome is extremely positive. It's tempting to want to swing things in favor of the querent, especially if you know them personally, but the cards just tell it like it is, and your job as a reader is to relay that message. If a reading looks good but the outcome comes with a warning, you're not doing anyone any favors by not bringing it up. Things can't always go our way. The best thing we can do is learn to roll with it and be prepared.

The Celtic Cross
Now we come to the quintessential spread, the Celtic Cross. This spread is the go-to for many readers because of how simple but dense it is. It can reveal an amazing amount of information once you get used to reading it.

The Celtic Cross consists of ten cards. 1 goes in the middle. 2 crosses over 1. 3 goes to the left of the 1-2 cross. 4 is above, 5 below. 6 is on the right. 7, 8, 9, and 10 form a vertical line to the right of cards 1-6. So the shape you should have is a cross within a larger cross with a straight border going up the right side.

1 and 2 represent the crux of the question as of the present moment. 1 is the main influence, and with 2, you have what challenges that.

3 shows past influences that have brought this present into effect.

4 is the energy over the situation, the conscious factor.

5 is the foundation of the reading, the root cause of the situation, the unconscious impulses.

6 is the immediate future if things continue as they are.

The querent's thoughts and feelings about the situation are shown in 7.

The environment around the question is 8.

9 is hopes and fears of the querent about the circumstances.

10 is the most important card, the Outcome card. This card is the key to the situation.

The Celtic Cross can be used for just about any question. However, it's best used if you want a very thorough reading, so it's not recommended if you're strapped for time or just want a quick answer.

The Celtic Cross is also a great spread if you want to keep diving even deeper into the reading. Like we talked about in the Cross spread, sometimes the outcome card seems to go against the rest of the reading, for better or worse. If that happens, a good thing to do is to take that outcome card and make it the center of another reading.

Place the other nine cards back into the deck for shuffling, and place the outcome in the 1 position. When you choose your first card like this, it's known as the significator. Some readers like to do this for every reading by choosing a card that best represents the question or the querent, but in this case, the significator was chosen for you by being the outcome of the last reading.

Your question as you shuffle should be about expanding on this card, asking for clarification, and how the card relates to the original question in more detail. Then you begin your reading by laying down the 2 card crossing the significator, and so on from there.

Decision Spread
Another very useful one is the Decision spread. This is designed to help the querent make a choice between two options.

You lay down your 1 card, which is you or the querent.

To the right, you're going to lay out six cards in two rows. Cards 2, 3, and 4 will be the top row, and 5, 6, and 7 finish off the reading on the bottom row.

The two rows show the choices at hand, each displaying the sequential order of events that might play out down each path if that choice is taken. If there are more than two choices, simply add further rows to signify the other possibilities.

If you want to get more out the Decision spread, do it again, but this time focus on one option. The top row becomes what will happen if you make this choice, and the bottom one is what will happen if you don't. Then repeat for the second choice. This way, by repeating the spread from a different angle of the same question, you gain more insight into what is the best option for you.

Deck Interview
One spread that is good to do with new decks you acquire is the Deck Interview spread. This spread is specifically to talk to your deck directly. It's been mentioned before in this book that many people consider their decks to have their own distinct personalities, and this spread was designed to help you tap into that personality and draw it out to let it speak for itself. So while you're shuffling, as the deck itself, "What do I need to know about you? What are your strengths and weaknesses? How can we best work together?"

Put down six cards. You can lay them out in a line, in a circle, or in two rows. The shape of the spread for this one doesn't really matter as long as there are six cards and you know in what order you put them down.

Card 1 is the deck's defining characteristic.

2 is the deck's strengths.

3 is its weaknesses.

4 is about what the deck wants to teach you.

5 is how best to work with the deck.

6 is the outcome of this relationship.

Don't be surprised if you get some astonishingly sassy answers, especially if you're talking to a deck you've had some difficulty working with already. The decks will let you know what they want to be used for. Some decks actually don't want to be used so much for divination but instead want to mine into the psyche and bring guidance for bigger, more spiritual questions. Some will reveal that they're rather secretive and won't give you all the information you need in a reading, preferring you figure it out for yourself. Others will be quite blunt.

If you've been having trouble with a deck, this spread really helps open that door of communication so you can better understand your deck.

Johari Window
This spread is based on an actual psychological test called the Johari window, which helps people evaluate how they relate to themselves and others around them. We're going to keep the basic shape and principle, but in this case, instead of filling out a blank, you'll insert the answer with the tarot.

This spread is four cards laid down to form a square, like the panes in a window. There's only one question to ask for this one: "What are the known and unknown parts about myself?"

Card 1 is what's open—what you know about yourself that others know about you as well.

2 is your blind spot. This is what you don't know about yourself that others see.

3 is what you hide. This is what you know but others do not know about you.

The last, 4, is the unknown, which is the deeper elements of yourself that neither you nor anyone else is aware of.

This is a spread that should be used sparingly. It's deeply insightful and can be useful to help you figure out your feelings if you're going through a troubling transition and need to reconnect with yourself. But because it's so specific and penetrating, it shouldn't become a standard reading you use weekly for practice. It is a great conversation starter, though, if you decide to use it on someone else.

Chakra Reading
Chakras are a Hindu concept describing energy centers running along the spine that determine how balanced our spiritual selves are. In order to do this reading, it helps to be familiar with these and how each chakra affects you. If you already understand the basic concept, go ahead and try out this spread.

For this one, the question will be, "What are the energies of my chakras?" You're going to lay out seven cards in a vertical line. Each of these cards is going to correspond to a chakra. 1 is the Root. 2 is the Sacral, 3 is the Solar Plexus. 4 is the Heart. 5 is the Throat. 6 is the Third Eye. 7 is the Crown.

Through this spread, you'll get a visual of how each of your chakras is functioning. Often, this will enlighten you as to which ones are way out of balance and which ones are completely blocked.

An alternative question to ask is, "How can I balance and unblock my chakras?" Then your reading will tell you what work specifically needs to be done to help each chakra.

The Golden Dawn Spread
This spread was developed by the Order of the Golden Dawn for use with its very specific philosophy regarding the meaning and symbolism of each card. As such, it's a little more of a challenge to read. Much like the Decision spread, it can also be used to help a querent make a choice, or if the querent even has a choice at all.

There are fifteen cards in this card, laid out in five groups of three. The first group is the middle of the reading. The other four form corners around this middle group. To lay down the cards, you put 1 in the middle, 2 to the left of it, then 3 to the right. Then you lay out the other cards by starting at the upper right-hand group, and circling counterclockwise to the upper left, then lower left, then lower right, coming back around to the upper right, working from the inner to the outer cards, until all fifteen have been placed.

So in the middle, you have cards 2-1-3. In the upper left-hand group, you get cards 13-9-5. The upper right-hand are cards 4-8-12. Lower left is 14-10-6. The lower right holds 7-11-15.

2-1-3 represents the querent. It is the central trinity to the reading. This tells you the most direct influences on the question as it regards the querent and really gets into the heart of the matter. These three cards can be read in any order, but usually it's approached as the middle card, 1, is the main card of the querent themselves, with 2 and 3 winging it as side influences.

4-8-12 is the querent's current path. This shows the sequence of events as they will play out if the querent continues on as they are.

13-9-5 is the alternative path. This is the choice the querent faces, the other sequence of events that might happen if the querent decides to go a different way.
However, this is where this particular spread gets interesting. If 4-8-12 and 13-9-5 seem to be relaying the same message, then the spread is telling you that the querent doesn't really have a choice on the issue they're asking about. There is only one path for them

to take. In which case, 13-9-5 isn't an alternative path, but a continuation of the sequence of events laid out in 4-8-12. So the chronological order is read as the right trinity, then the left trinity.

4-10-6 forms the psychological basis of the reading. This is what's going on in the querent's mind and what they are thinking about the question at hand. Much like the middle trinity, these three can be read in any order, but usually with the middle first, followed by the other two as influencing factors

7-11-15 is the querent's karma. These are read like the querent and psychological basis groups. These cards hold the key to why things are the way they are in regards to the question. This tells you what the querent might be carrying around with them, or what attitudes or beliefs they've held that have led to the present. This is crucial because what attitude you have will invariably attract the same.

This spread can be read very freely. Usually, the reader will interpret the middle group first since it's the core of the reading, but after that, you can follow the others around and allow your intuition to guide you from one group to the next. This gives an incredibly expansive reading.

The Bottom Card
Another layer you can add to your reading is to look at the card on the bottom of your deck after you lay out your cards. This is isn't something every reader does, but some swear by it. Readers interpret the bottom card in different ways.

For some, it sets the theme of the reading, suggesting the overarching message that can bring everything together. To others, the bottom card can be considered to be what's hidden in a reading, what is just out of sight but affecting the situation. Another way to read it is as a 'not about' card, where the bottom card tells you what the issue is not about. This can really help with a difficult reading as it nudges you away from obvious preconceptions and to think more carefully about what you're looking at.

Clarifiers
In a difficult reading, clarifiers can help you bring a muddy issue into focus. Clarifiers are extra cards you pull to expound upon the

main cards of the layout. For example, say you have a three-card spread. You've figured out what the present and future cards mean, but the past card has you stumped. In that case, clarifiers help to bring the message into focus. You can pull clarifiers straight off the top of the deck as-is. Reshuffling the deck with the intent of clarifying the card in question is also an option. Start with one or two, but don't be afraid to pull more until you understand what the card is trying to say.

It's important to note, though, that clarifiers should be used as a last resort after you've taken the time to study the spread and tried to figure it out on your own. If used too often, it becomes a crutch, and you don't develop the intuition needed to effectively read the cards. We'll discuss how to read with intuition more in Chapter 9.

It's important to keep in mind that spreads are fluid. It's okay if you don't lay the cards in strictly sequential order. If it feels right to lay them down differently, it won't affect your reading. Even disregarding the meanings of each placement and going instead with a more structure-less approach is fine, if you are confident enough to do so. These spreads are merely a guide to help you glean what the cards are trying to say. You can also create your own if you don't find one you like. Some readers are traditionalists and like to use the tried-and-true methods, while others are more free-form. Both approaches reflect the intuition of the reader and are perfectly acceptable ways to read tarot.

You can also combine spreads to work together. For example, if you do a three-card reading and get an answer that seems much more complicated than just what those three cards say, use them to expand into a nine-card reading. Or, you can change the shape entirely. Take those three cards and add two more to make a Cross. If that's still not enough, build it into a Celtic Cross. You can even build a Golden Dawn spread out of a simple three-card spread as its base. The important thing is, keep going until you can get the full picture.

If you have more than one deck, you can use both decks to help each other. With one deck you might have a Celtic Cross, then use another deck for an additional three-card reading that helps clarify some things. You can even combine different divination decks outside of tarot, like Lenormand or oracle cards. Some readers will make a nine-card spread with tarot, then pull one or two oracle cards to give them additional advice on what tarot has already said. This approach to reading can be very fun and experimental, but it might be best to hold off on trying this until you are comfortable with the tarot on its own.

It's important to remember the notion of free will in all of this. Whatever your beliefs, when you do a reading for a querent, always preface your reading by reassuring them that this reading is only a window into the situation. It's like a snapshot taken of the present moment that allows study into the details of what's going on. It is not an unshakable prediction that will come true no matter what. Everyone has the ability to change their lives, and the tarot's best purpose is to allow people to see how they can bring about that change for themselves. If a reading veers negative, the best thing to do for your querent, or even for yourself, is to suggest a call to action. Use the cards to enable them to make positive steps for themselves. Don't sugar-coat everything but give practical advice. The best way to handle the truth is to use the truth to your advantage.

That should be enough to give you some ideas on what spreads you want to try for yourself. Let's move on to how to interpret the meanings of the cards within the context of a reading.

CHAPTER 8
Reading With Context

Every card has an essential meaning to it. However, the power of the tarot is in how those essential meanings are woven together to create a story. Their position in a spread will affect how it reads, and they influence each other in a spread. More than anything, though, the true defining factor of reading is the question. The entire context of a reading is determined by that one thing alone.

For example, if the Two of Cups shows up in a reading, it does not always mean romance, even though that is its primary meaning. In a career reading, it would not make sense to read it that way since the question is about work, not love. So you have to put the card's message into context. In this case, the Two of Cups in a career reading can show a partnership with a peer that flows easily and helps build productivity. Or ideas that are coming together to form a cohesive project. If you were to ask about money, the Two of Cups' meaning adapts again, this time serving as a reassurance that you have the emotional support you need to get through troubling times. The meaning of a card has to be applied to the question and not taken at literal face value.

To demonstrate this, let's create a practice reading. Take your cards and lay them out for yourself, if you like. We're going to do a three-card spread since it's simple but enough to illustrate the points we want to make here. We'll have the Seven of Pentacles for the left card, Strength in the middle, and the Knight of Cups on the right.

Now we'll apply a series of different questions to these three cards. The first question we'll ask is a common one. "When will the one I marry come into my life?" If you have the cards laid out, take a moment to try and answer this question yourself. Refer back to the previous chapters covering the card meanings and try to put them together within the question.

Don't worry about if your answer right or wrong—since this is hypothetical, it's hard to be right or wrong anyway. This is just for practice, and to show you how the cards are read together with fluidity rather than stunted 'this is this and that is that.'

Now here's the interpretation we'll give in his book. The Seven of Pentacles means slow progress and taking the long-term view. Strength is personal will. The Prince of Cups is the energy of someone or something that is passionate and driven by creativity or emotions. How do these apply to the question?

The Seven of Pentacles in the past position shows the querent as someone who feels on the edge of failure, who fears they will never meet the spouse they desire. The querent has put a lot of time and effort into relationships in the past but has yet to find anything truly rewarding and feels like they're not getting anywhere.

In the present, though, with the presence of Strength, this shows that the querent is really trying to gather their strength and overcome their feelings of disappointment. In terms of advice, as the Major Arcana, Strength is strongly pointing out this is a good thing about them and encouraging the querent to focus on their strength as an individual and to find personal satisfaction in themselves.

The Knight of Cups in the future is very good tidings for a romantic reading. Cups rule the heart, and Knights are things in motion. This likely indicates that someone may enter their lives who will be the weak-kneed, moony-eyed romance the querent desires.

To bring the reading together a short statement, you can read these three cards as, "Despite misgivings and set-backs from previous dating experiences, you have the fortitude within you to never give up. Recognize that in yourself and build up your confidence. That self-love will attract the person best suited for you."

Of course, this is just an example. Again, if you got something different, it's not necessarily right or wrong. This reading would depend on the querent's personality and individual situation. But hopefully, this illustrates the basics of how to weave the cards together.

Notice also that even though this is a 'when' question, the tarot does not give a specific time. Some talented psychics can intuit that information, but usually, the tarot is not very good for time frames.

The tarot likes to explore the psyche and give guidance, so instead of giving a practical answer, it tells you the sequence of events as they need to unfold for you to find what you're looking for. When will the one show up? The short answer, when you learn to love yourself. With no specific timeline, this can be very far-reaching into the future. If you want to know if something is going to happen within a certain time, that must be specified in the question.

Here's another question for these three cards. "How can I find the career best suited for me?"

In this case, since the question is about a job, the Seven of Pentacles is leaning more towards the material aspect of the Pentacles. Since the Seven is so dragged down, this shows that the job the querent has been working has not felt worthwhile. They feel they are going nowhere, or even that it does not pay enough for the work they put into it.

Strength shows the empowerment that comes from that realization. Recognizing that you're not where you want to be is a powerful thing. But it's only the first step in figuring out what you do want. Strength here shows that the querent has to use their energy towards finding the path they want for themselves. They need to realize they have power over their own lives.

The Knight of Cups likely represents the querent here. They need to embody that energy to move forward. The Knight of Cups follows his passions. This shows that the querent will find the way to their dream career will be open to them if they take action on it.

All together, the message here is, "Your career is unfulfilling and only holding you back. Realize you have power over your own life, and free yourself to pursue your dreams."

Let's do one more. "What is standing in the way of my optimal health?"

The Seven of Pentacles shows a sluggishness. There's definitely an indication there's been lack of exercise on the part of the querent.

Strength here could be literal physicality. Combined with the Seven of Pentacles' lack of exercise, this seems to be saying some sort of strength training would be beneficial to the querent. So going to the gym would be the best step towards optimal health.

Just to practice, let's say you get to the Knight of Cups and are stumped. He deals with emotions and creativity, so what is he doing here in a reading about physical health? You draw a clarifier for that card and get the Emperor. What does this say about the Knight of Cups? The Emperor is all about rules and governance. The Knight of Cups is characterized by dreaminess. Being Major Arcana, the Emperor then is emphasizing that tendency in the Knight and creating a contrast.

With the Emperor guiding interpretation, we can see what the Knight of Cups is saying is not to get distracted by ideals but to focus on the self-discipline and hard work it will take to reach your health goals. Strength next to it only bolsters this.

In a nutshell, "It's lack of exercise that's keeping you from your best self. Go to the gym and work out. Keep it up and don't let yourself get distracted by pie-in-the-sky goals. Focus on what's realistically healthy for you."

Let's ask the first question again with three different cards, just to illustrate this process again. This time, let's have the Two of Swords on the left, Three of Pentacles in the middle, and the Wheel of Fortune to the right.

We'll also modify the first question a bit with a narrower time frame. "Will the one I marry come into my life within the next year?"

The Two of Swords shows indecision. In regards to this question, it's likely the querent has become guarded against others and tries not to put any real thought into relationships so they don't have to open up to anyone. Since this question is now within a time frame, the Two may also be indicating a delay.

The Three of Pentacles is about cooperation and work. This means the querent really wants someone who's down for the dirty work of building a life together. With the time frame in mind, Pentacles are always slow-moving, even when they show progress, which emphasizes the delay of the Two of Swords.

The Wheel of Fortune is fate and the passage of time. Again, this is showing the ticking of the clock. But it also brings a message of patience, of knowing that there will be a spouse for the querent. Being a Major Arcana, it pretty much guarantees it will happen—when the time is right.

So the concise answer is, "This partner is unlikely to arrive in the next year. There are barriers that have to come down in you. Work needs to be done on figuring out what life you want to create for yourself so you can open up to that partnership. It may take a while, but that person is coming, and they will be more than worth the wait."

If you got something else out of it when you read your cards, keep in mind there's no definitive right or wrong, especially since this is just an exercise and there is no actual querent. This is just to demonstrate an example of how the questions truly gathers the meaning of the cards and how they play off each other. As long as you practice, that's what really matters for now.

An important part of the way they affect each other is determining when a card's shadow aspect is being brought into play. Ill-dignified cards, called shadow aspect in this book, is when a card's negative or opposite traits come to the surface due to the influence of the cards around it. We already did this in an above reading, with the Knight of Cups in regards to the question, "What is standing in the way of my optimal health?" While he was a positive card in a question of romance or a career, in regards to health, the Knight of Cups came forward to show his negative qualities of distraction and lofty ideals, which do not work when the question is about attaining realistic results physically.

Some readers do this through what is known as reversals, which is when a card is drawn upside-down. This is a helpful way to indicate when a card is in shadow aspect. Reversals can also mean that the card's energies are blocked and need to be unlocked. On some occasions, reversals emphasize the card's meaning to make sure you pay attention to it. As always, this is determined by the context of the reading.

Let's set up another three-card spread. This time, we'll ask a more serious question. "Should I end my relationship?" Draw the cards the World, the Page of Swords, and the Five of Wands. But this time, turn the World into the reversed position. Pretend for this exercise that it came out of the deck upside-down since you usually don't turn cards in reverse during a reading if they weren't laid out that way straight from the deck.

Now, what does the World show us in reverse? The World usually talks about wholeness and the element of the change that can come from things coming to completion. In reverse, there are several things that could be going on. That energy could be blocked, meaning that change is trying to influence the reading but isn't able to. It could be showing the card's shadow aspect, which would be inertia or permanence and things standing still because nothing has fully come together. Or it could be emphasizing its message, saying it's very important to embrace the World's energy.

Which is it? The answer lies in the other cards as they relate to the question.

So let's look at the other two cards. The Page of Swords card brings discernment into the reading, and the ability to resolve disputes. All the Court cards in the Swords suit are about using your head, not your heart. The Five of Wands is a card of strife, but being able to overcome them if you put your effort into it. As they relate to the World in reverse, they seem to be working in tandem to bring out the World as a lack of cohesion or forward movement. So in the past, the World reversed says that in this relationship, there was a feeling of being stuck and incomplete. In regards to how the querent feels, it suggests they don't want to leave the relationship despite their concerns. Being a Major Arcana, this is the strongest message in the reading.

To sum it up, "This relationship has reached an impasse, and yet there is a strong feeling that you don't want to call it quits just yet. It will take significant effort to rectify the issues if you really want to make it work. You need to think about it and discern the problems for what they are and not just how they make you feel. It will be a struggle to solve them, but if you and your partner are willing to slog it out and confront them, you will be able to work it out."

Being able to read ill-dignified or reversed cards will come much easier with practice. Once you get comfortable with the process, sometimes the reversed cards will help clarify right-side up cards instead. It all comes down to practice, and opening up your intuition.

CHAPTER 9
The Role Of Intuition

Memorizing card meanings is one thing. Grasping how to read them is another. While being able to context them logically is a big part of the skill of tarot reading, the art of tarot is the use of your intuition.

We've mentioned intuition several times already during the course of this book. It permeates everything about tarot. The point of the imagery and the use of allegorical figures to describe our universe to is tap into our capacity for metaphor, which is at the heart of our cultures, our stories, and our dreams. By linking themselves to our subconscious language, the tarot opens us up to our intuitions, and through that gives the answers to our most pressing questions.

Every person has an intuition. For some, it is much more developed. Some people were born with it already strong while others have to work on it, much like how some people are born gifted at math and others need tutoring to pass algebra. But just about everyone can think of at least one point in their lives where they had a feeling about something that turned out to be correct despite there being no logical reason they should know. This is a phenomenon often experienced by parents, who have such strong intuitive bonds to their children that they simply know something is wrong even when their child is out of sight. Usually, these types of stories are prefaced with, "I don't know why I thought to do that," or, "I don't know how I knew," or, "I just got a got a feeling."

That 'feeling' is what the tarot trains you to tap into. For all the logic and memorization that goes into learning the cards and reading them in context, the real reading comes from that intuitive voice.

A lot of this can be done by learning to look at the images on your tarot cards. It's common for beginners to lay out their cards and look up the meanings of the cards, and string them together from there. It's what we did in the preceding chapter when talking about context, and this is a legitimate way to do a reading, especially when you're learning. It's how pip cards were originally read before the Rider-Waite made it popular to illustrate them.

But in text, it's impossible to get across the importance of the art on the tarot decks. This is why getting a deck you respond to visually so key to reading well. The meanings of the cards remain the same across all decks. But you might get a different intuitive reading from one deck than you would from another, simply because the images for the same cards would be different.

Very often, the tarot communicates so much in the images drawn for a reading. It's not just the meaning of the cards, it's also the figures in the cards. What are they doing? What are they wearing? Do you see patterns in the cards in the overall reading? With tarot, the big picture can often tell you a lot more than getting lost in the minutiae of what a card is supposed to mean. The card's meaning according to the book absolutely informs the reading, but if you feel drawn to a card specifically because the figure in the card is doing something that attracts your interest, that's your intuition telling you that card is important.

Intuition will also help you expand your readings. You might get an intuitive nudge during a reading that tells you that there's more to the question than meets the eye. Maybe the querent doesn't fully trust you and is withholding information, or perhaps the right questions weren't asked in the first place. But during your reading, there are a couple of cards that really stand out to you, and don't seem to be resolved within the spread. You can reshuffle the cards and ask about those specific cards, and you'll likely find the answers in the next spread. But it takes intuition to know that.

Unfortunately, a book can't exactly teach you how to use your intuition. It's something you have to grasp for yourself. When you sense your intuition, you'll know it, but the process can only be felt. However, we can provide exercises to help you key in and nurture it.

The first thing you can do for your intuition is to meditate, meditate, meditate. Both spirituality and science have proclaimed to the high heavens how healthy this is for the mind, so what are you waiting for? Even just five to ten minutes a day will help you feel more relaxed and focused. In regards to your intuition, meditation taps into the part of the brain where intuition speaks most clearly. If your intuition can speak clearly, then it can direct you through your tarot readings more effectively.

Meditate during a time of the day when you're most awake, so not right before bed and not right after waking up. Sit anywhere that's comfortable but also allows you to sit up straight. You want your spine aligned so your physical energy is flowing even while the rest of you is relaxed. Close your eyes, and breathe deeply. Counting your breaths helps, usually in a pattern of breathing in for three counts, holding it for three, then letting out in three counts. In through the nose and out through the mouth. You can do this for the entire five minutes, but in order to enter the meditative mindset, you only need to count for a handful of breaths.

The trick with meditation is to try and not think about anything in particular. Thoughts will come and go, but it's best to visualize them as clouds floating by. Our mind usually wants to grab onto thoughts and follow them endlessly, but in meditation, you let them go. The thought appears, then it floats off. Eventually, as you get more experienced with this, meditation will become a space of silence. You'll be able to induce a mental state where there are no thoughts, just a peaceful calm where your mind can fully unwind.

You don't even realize just how hard your work your mind all the time until you relax it, like when you get a hand massage and you feel the muscles in your palms and fingers lost their tension. By allowing the mind to relax, not only will it work its logical processes more effectively, but it will also increase the more psychic capabilities like intuition.

This leads into the next way you can tune into your intuition. As you meditate more often, you'll find you're more attentive and more aware of the space around you. Focus on that awareness, and let the moment truly sink in. Be aware of all the sounds in the room. Notice the colors around you, in the rug, on your chair, out the window. Look at the quality of the light, and take the time to appreciate shadows created by the light. Notice your physical form, how it feels sitting where it is.

This is called being present in the moment. Let thoughts come and go, but don't hold onto them. The past isn't the present. The future can't be fully known beyond the present. The most important moment is now, and the now is where the intuition resides. In the now, there is no depression about the past. In the now, there are no anxieties about the future. All that matters is the now, and all the running thoughts you have about what you're doing and what you're not doing and what you should be doing stops in the appreciation of where you are exactly this moment, and who you are as a full, whole human being in this moment.

Similar to meditation, taking the time to be present in the moment should be done every day. When you allow your consciousness to leave the constant chatter of your mind and spread out into the world like that, even if only for a few moments at a time, you're opening the door to allowing your intuition to flow forth. That constant chatter usually overrides the intuition because it's so loud and never seems to stop running, and it's screaming about things that aren't anymore or things that might happen. Neither of these is the present reality, and they only serve to drown out the intuition.

Once you get a feel for what your intuition feels like, you can perform more active practices to strengthen it. For example, keeping a 'hunch' journal. Here, you write down any feelings you have about things. Do you get the feeling that it might rain tomorrow? Do you have a hunch about someone you just met at work? Did you turn on the TV to a game show and sense one particular contestant will win? Write these hunches down, and refer back to them later to see if you were right. Eventually, you'll be able to tell the difference between when it's your intuition truly speaking to you, and when it's your logical brain throwing out possible projections.

It's also good to spend time with just your intuition. This is a similar process to meditation in that you're sitting still and closing your eyes, but instead of trying to let all thoughts flow away to attain a state of perfect calm, intuitive meditation is when you open the floodgates to your intuition and pay attention to the visions and impressions that come out. Sit with it for a few minutes a day, and write down your impressions. Did you see certain colors? Or a scene, like a landscape or a room? Did you see a face, and was it someone you know or someone you've never seen before? What feeling did you get from any of these? Record them, and then write down if you see these visions revealed in real life.

Take note, though, that just seeing something in real life that your intuition revealed to you does not mean it's an important vision that's going to affect the course of your life. What it means is that you're working out that intuitive muscles. Your intuition is reaching out further and further and picking up on details that you otherwise would've missed. It's helping you to connect the external and the internal so they can work in tandem. If you make your intuition strong, then when something important is on the horizon, there will be no mistaking it. You'll know it instantly.

The same can be said of your tarot readings. Between meditation and being in the now, you'll train your brain to slow down, take a breath, and assess what's really happening in reality and not what you think might happen. This head space is the key to reading with intuition. To look at the cards and instead of thinking, "This is what this *should* mean," you read the cards and just let the intuition opened by meditation and the present moment guide your thoughts.

CHAPTER 10
Exercises & Practice

The best thing you can do to get better at reading tarot is to practice every day. You can read for yourself, obviously, but you'll get to a point where you run out of questions, or you start repeating. And as every experienced tarot reader knows, if you repeat questions over and over, the cards tend to get a bit huffy and stop answering. They gave you their answer, now quit asking.

You run into the same problem if you read for family or friends. Everyone's got problems, but once you do a reading on that problem, you'll start hitting roadblocks if you try to over-extrapolate. You also wouldn't want to wish ill on your loved ones just to have something to do a reading about.

So in lieu of having specific questions to ask or anyone to practice on, here are some techniques you can use to keep going and work out that card-reading intuitive muscle.

Daily Draw
So if there's no one around to read, how can you continue to practice? Probably the best way is to do what's known as a daily draw. You ask the tarot, "What is my message for today?" Then draw one card. This is really good to do at the end of the day when you've already had all your trials and tribulations. Then the card allows you to think over the events of the day and reflect.

It's a good idea to keep a journal for this, especially when you're learning. At the start, write down the meanings of the card as a bullet-point list, to help you retain the information. Then meditate on the card, look at its message, and keep your mind open to any words, thoughts, and images that flow in. Write down what the message you're receiving through the tarot means to you. Not only does this allow you to use your logical brain to memorize and apply a specific definition to the events of your day, but it also opens up your intuitive mind to get more information.

If you're having a difficult time opening up to your intuition, visualization helps. Look at the image of the tarot card you drew for the day. Study it, and take a closer look at the details on the card. What's the first thing you notice? What does the mood of the figures seem to be? What's going on in the background? And most importantly, what is your gut reaction? Write all that down too, and get into the nitty-gritty as you feel like.

With the card now firmly in your mind, close your eyes. In your mind, keep the image of the tarot card first and foremost. Often your mind will try to bring in different images to supersede it, but that's normal. It takes practice to hold the card there. Then, allow the tarot card to move in your mind. Animate it, allow it to break free of the confines of the card dimensions, and see what it does without directing it. Very often, the actions the figures in the cards take as you're visualizing them will give you a clue as to why this card came up for you, and how it applies to your day. Write down what you see, and then interpret.

You can also practice the one-card visualization technique with a more specific question. If you're doing a reading for yourself, it's a good idea to do this before laying down a spread. It helps lead you into the spread by already giving you an idea of how to piece together what you're about to read. With enough practice, you'll be able to do this without a tarot card as an aid, and simply open your mind to what your intuition can attune to.

Journaling your reads, in general, is so important, especially as you're starting out. You'd be amazed how much leaves your head when the reading ends. If you write down your impressions and predictions, and when you are further along in your studies, you can go back over your entries and see how far you've come. This is an invaluable gift to give your future self. Since it's just for you, there's no right or wrong. This is just a reflection. You get out of it only what you need to. Eventually, you won't need to write down every little thing. You'll have the cards memorized, and your intuition will be honed to where impressions will come fluidly to you. Then you can write about your daily draw freely and easily.

Using the News
But just reflecting on your day or meditating doesn't sound super exciting, you say. This is divination. You want to know if you can predict the future.

If you want to test your predictive skills, there's no better way than to do readings on the news and current events. This is information that can be verified easily, and if it's a big story, it'll be hard to miss it as it unfolds. So if there's a breaking news story, after you read up on the details, take the time to do a reading on it. You can ask specific questions about it, especially if you've got that intuitive feeling about it. But sometimes the news can take a while to wrap up, so another way to approach it if you're impatient is to simply ask how the situation will unfold within the next two weeks. Then you have a short time frame in which to wait.

The best thing about this technique is how objective you can be about it. Sometimes, if you're reading for yourself or someone you're close to, it can be hard to maintain enough emotional distance to give an honest reading. You want the best, and your wants can cloud what is as you're interpreting the cards. In the case of public current events, you're not emotionally close to the center of the reading, so it's easier to see the cards as they are.

It will also give you a good idea of how varied some of the cards can be when it comes to applying them to a reading. Usually what goes on in the news spans beyond the usual personal questions of love or careers. What a card like the Knight of Wands can mean will be a lot different for a larger, perhaps more political question than you'd ever get out of your own inquiries.

If you do readings on the news, make sure to write down your predictions with the date. That way you can refer back to what you read in the cards. Another good idea is to draw out the spread from that reading. That way, if you got a prediction wrong, you can go back to the reading and go over what cards were there, and get a sense of which ones you may have misinterpreted.

Party Trick
The most obvious way to practice is to go read for a wide variety of people. If you're not in a business already, which we can assume not if you're just beginning, then how would you find strangers to practice on? One easy way is to take your deck when you go to a party or barbecue and offer to read for anyone who's interested.

Obviously, doing this requires some confidence, so you're not ready right out the gate to do this, that's okay. Take whatever time you need to build up your skills to where you're comfortable with this. There might also be an element of embarrassment about it as if being interested in the tarot is weird and people might think it odd. It's undeniable that some might, but you'd be surprised just how many people are keen to get a reading, especially if it's free. Most are more than happy to be your guinea pigs if you're honest about it and say right out the gate it's for practice. It might also help you connect with others and maybe even make a few friends, as tarot has a tendency to get people to open up and be more honest with themselves and with you as the reader.

Card Clubs
Finding other people who are interested in the tarot and may have more experience is important for the development of your reading skills. While books such as this one can offer a great base knowledge, there's nothing to replace actual human conversation and insight.

With the resurgence of popularity in the tarot, there are many tarot clubs forming. Especially in more developed areas, there are usually metaphysical shops that not only serve as a store but usually also offer space for workshops and weekly groups. If there is a metaphysical shop in your area, it's worth going in and talking to the staff to see if they offer anything like that, or at least if they know of any group focused on the tarot in the area.

If there is no club already formed in your area, create one yourself! It can be pretty easy to find other interested parties to build up a group. Facebook is probably the easiest way to connect with your community, but if you'd rather go about it more anonymously, Craigslist has a board for events where you can post the details and see who shows up. Simple paper posts at metaphysical shops or on a community board might seem old-fashioned but these boards still get a lot of marketing traffic, and you'd be surprised at the number of people who respond to these.

A word of caution, though: there are people out there who like to take the mickey out of psychics and tarot readers. If you advertise too widely, you might end up attracting people who only want to come to make fun of everyone else there. It's an unpleasant fact of life, but something you should be aware of if you want to create an open community for spiritualists.

An easy way to dissuade this behavior is to have a fee for every meeting, something minimal like $5. Usually, people who aren't that serious about it will leave it at that, preferring to go waste their time somewhere else rather than spend the money. As for people who are genuine, this money can either be returned to them later, or it can be pooled together as a resource for the group to buy supplies, or plan an event, or rent a better space to have meetings. Whatever works best for the group you have.

Online Resources
Another way to find more spreads, more exercises and more advice on how to continue getting better with your tarot practice is to look online.

As mentioned in Chapter 2, there are a lot of tarot forums available online. It was brought up there as a way to find indie decks not widely available, but an online community is a ripe source of discussion and ideas that can set your imagination on fire and make you itch to try something new. Facebook hosts dozens of group forums based around tarot, but there are independent sites out there where tarot is the entire focus.

YouTube is also full of channels dedicated to tarot. Some are specifically meant to serve as teaching guides, so looking up videos to explore the concepts set out in this book may help you understand further what was introduced here.

Other channels are simply filmed readings, one popular format being the pick-a-card reading. This is when the readers will set out pre-drawn piles of cards to answer the question posed in the video. Then those who watch the videos pick the pile they feel drawn to and get a reading. Obviously, since these are pre-filmed and meant for a general audience, they're very broad and may not always resonate. However, they can be tools to help you understand how different readers find meaning in their cards, what different kinds of spreads can be used, and how to bring a reading together. You might even get an unexpected helpful message along the way.

It is also very popular among tarot readers online to use the news as a means to get traffic on their channel, much like we discussed earlier in this chapter. This can be helpful to you if you choose to practice your cards that way since their videos can be used to compare and contrast what you're getting when you read about the same question.

CONCLUSION

Now you've made it to the end of the book. Congratulations! You have learned a lot since you started.

Hopefully, this text has provided you with all the tools you need to get started with the tarot. You've gained an understanding of the individual cards, learned all the various ways you can combine them in a spread, and then how to interpret their meaning using both contextual logic and intuition. Now all you need to do is practice, practice, practice.

Try as many techniques as you can. Not just what was laid out here, either, but also anything else you find. Tarot is an evolving journey, so your methods will perfect over time and grow and change as you grow and change as a reader. What works today as a novice might be useless a year from now when you've learned even more from other tarot practitioners. Allow yourself these changes. Listen to your own guidance alongside that of others. Tune more fully into your intuition, and your abilities will only grow.

The last thing to touch as a conclusion is to remind you that, at the end of the day, the cards are just cards. They seem to have a life of their own at times, and especially if you study up on the more esoteric aspects of it, they can grow to mean much more than as a pack of pretty art. But in all of this, you need to keep in mind that you have free will. No matter what the cards say, you have a life to live. It's easy when you get into tarot to use it too much to the exclusion of making decisions or thinking through things on your own. This is not what the tarot is meant for. It is a guide, an advisor when things seem overwhelming, a way to focus your mind and come up with a creative approach to life's challenges. Do not use it as a crutch, or think you need it to get by.

Your life is your own. The tarot is only here to help you live it to its potential.

If you enjoyed this book, please take the time to rate it on Amazon. An honest review would be greatly appreciated. You're part of the tarot community now! Your feedback helps others on their journey to find spiritual enlightenment. Thank you, and good luck with your readings!

DESCRIPTION FOR BOOK

Tarot carries with it an image of mystique. When most hear the word, they think of psychic clairvoyance and prophecies foretelling the weight of destiny.

But tarot is not as intimidating as one might think...

Tarot Reading for Beginners is a guide that removes the veil of that mystique and reveals the true nature of the tarot to anyone who wishes to learn. Drawing on the traditions laid down by the Order of the Golden Dawn, this is a comprehensive overview of the history and mythos of the tarot, its divinatory meanings, and how to use intuition and context to read the cards with masterful clarity.

Inside you will find
- Spiritual and divinatory meanings of the Major Arcana, so the cards can be used both for reading the future and as a tool for self-reflection
- An explanation of the numerical pip cards of the Minor Arcana using the framework of numerology
- An in-depth analysis of the Court cards of the Minor Arcana
- Historical context on where the cards came from, including exploring hermetic and Kabbalic influences
- A thorough explanation of how to read the cards for divination using the context of the question
- A series of easy spreads for you to try for yourself with explanations on how they work and what each spread is best suited for
- Exercises you can do to practice, and further resources to help you develop your new skills
- ***And more...***

With the tarot, you can become more than what you are. You can rise up into what you were meant to be. Allow this guide to show you how.

DESCRIPTION FOR AUDIO BOOK

Tarot carries with it an image of mystique. When most hear the word, they think of psychic clairvoyance and prophecies foretelling the weight of destiny.

But tarot is not as intimidating as one might think.

Tarot Reading for Beginners is a guide that removes the veil of that mystique and reveals the true nature of the tarot to anyone who wishes to learn. Drawing on the traditions laid down by the Order of the Golden Dawn, this is a comprehensive overview of the history and mythos of the tarot, its divinatory meanings, and how to use intuition and context to read the cards with masterful clarity.

It also explores the true intent of the tarot: as a spiritual tool to aid personal growth. The ancient, esoteric symbolism within the cards can lay a path of enlightenment for anyone who's willing to take the journey.

With the tarot, you can become more than what you are. You can rise up into what you were meant to be.

Allow this guide to show you how.

www.ingramcontent.com/pod-product-compliance
Lightning Source LLC
Chambersburg PA
CBHW071503070526
44578CB00001B/422